"A cinematographer himself, Sandler highlights techniques to aid visual storytelling from the first reading of the script to the shoot. He covers every visual tool in detail, from the direction and intensity of lighting, to the lenses and focus used. A brilliant read for those aspiring to be in his position."

—KATHRYN BUTT, *Raindance*

"This is one of the few books that covers why every facet of the picture is paramount. Sandler has created an indispensable, teachable guide for all filmmakers."

—DAVE WATSON, author, *Walkabout Undone*; editor, *Movies Matter*

"A golden guidebook that teaches you how to not only tell a great story, but how to draw your audience into your movie using what they see, more so than what they hear. Guides you through the techniques every filmmaker needs to know."

—FORRIS DAY JR., host, *Rolling Tape*; commentator, webseries *Hitch 20*

"Sandler's book is a clear and concise foundational text, a must read for any and all aspiring filmmakers. Covers the main components needed on the path to mastering the language of visual media."

—ROY FINCH, film professor, Chapman University

"Sandler's book is not only informative, but t look at the thought process behind every fr easy to understand way. This book should be maker and content creator."

—ERIC ENGLAND, director (*Contracted, Josie*)

"A 21st century skill set every communicator needs. This book weaves the basics with the art and craft of better visual communications. It should be the foundation of every class that teaches visual arts."

—CHRISTOPHER ZYDOWICZ, professor cinematic arts, Greenville, SC

"Succinct and engaging . . . this book succeeds in simplifying the complex technical world of filmmaking to digestible and relatable concepts while providing a fresh, candid and non-pretentious voice for the next generation of visual storytellers."

—VIKRAM M. JAYAKUMAR, writer, director (*Behind the Trees*)

"Sandler masterfully walks you through all the facets, tools and techniques that can make you a successful filmmaker. In clear detail he explains in a logical way how to successfully master your way through a film set. A definite must have."

—DANIEL STILLING, DFF, director of photography (*The Martian-NASA Unit, Priceless, Chasing Bullet*)

For Jillian, Stella and Eleanor, my reason for everything.

VISUAL STORYTELLING

HOW TO SPEAK TO YOUR AUDIENCE WITHOUT SAYING A WORD

MORGAN SANDLER

MICHAEL WIESE PRODUCTIONS

Published by Michael Wiese Productions
12400 Ventura Blvd. #1111
Studio City, CA 91604
(818) 379-8799, (818) 986-3408 (FAX)
mw@mwp.com
www.mwp.com

Cover design by Johnny Ink. www.johnnyink.com
Edited by David Wright
Interior design by William Morosi
Printed by McNaughton & Gunn

Manufactured in the United States of America

Library of Congress Cataloging-in-Publication Data

Names: Sandler, Morgan, 1980- author.
Title: Visual storytelling : how to speak to your audience without saying a
  word / Morgan Sandler.
Description: Studio City, CA : Michael Wiese Productions, [2018]
Identifiers: LCCN 2017056932 | ISBN 9781615932894
Subjects: LCSH: Storytelling in literature. | Narration (Rhetoric) | Visual
  literacy.
Classification: LCC PN56.S7357 .S26 2018 | DDC 791.4302--dc23
LC record available at https://lccn.loc.gov/2017056932

For Jillian, Stella and Eleanor, my reason for everything.

TABLE OF CONTENTS

TABLE OF CONTENTS

ACKNOWLEDGMENTS

ACKNOWLEDGMENTS

I would like to thank all of my students and colleagues at the University of La Verne and the many thousands of students I have had the pleasure of teaching over the years. It is your quest for knowledge that motivated me to write this book.

I would also like to thank Ryan Bartlett, Erik Boccio, Heather Fipps, Jamiel VanOver, Adam Hecker and Frank Leon for their hard work and dedication to this project. Without them this would not have been possible.

Thank you to my family and friends for their unwavering support. To my incredible wife Jillian and daughters Stella and Eleanor, thank you for your endless love and faith, you are my world. To my parents, Richard and Lorraine, grandparents Frank and Tina, and second parents, Jim and Mary, thank you for always believing in me. I love you all.

Lastly, a very special thank you to Margie Selke; the first person to make me believe that I could accomplish anything I set my mind to. You have changed my life in ways you will never know.

INTRODUCTION

INTRODUCTION

Although there are hundreds of books about the technical elements of filmmaking, this book takes a different approach. In this book we will examine how the technical elements of filmmaking affect the audience and create a deeper understanding of the story.

The concepts in this book will benefit writers, directors and cinematographers of all levels, and most importantly, give readers a strong foundation for telling a story visually. From aspiring filmmakers who have never touched a camera to seasoned veterans, there is something in this book for everyone.

For first-time filmmakers and film students, this book will serve as a complete guide to creating a well-crafted film and help you become a skilled filmmaker. Reading the book in chapter order will help you build upon your skills in a natural sequence and make the learning process feel organic.

For directors, the chapters on Composition, Camera Movement and Shooting Coverage will help you refine your skills, improve your technique and teach you how to use visual information to communicate with the audience, rather than just using dialogue.

For cinematographers, the chapters on the Camera as a Story-telling Tool, Lenses and Focus, and Lighting will help you improve your ability to bring the director's vision to life. Although many experienced filmmakers are comfortable with the technology, they don't always use it to its maximum potential. These chapters will change that.

As a film professor, I know firsthand the difficulty of creating curriculum for beginner filmmakers. I have structured this book correspondingly to my introductory and intermediate film classes and this book serves as an excellent accompaniment to those levels. Film instructors at both the high school and college level will find this book to be a useful companion to their teaching.

I have always seen film as a living, breathing thing that is always growing and changing. This means that no matter where you fall in the filmmaking spectrum, there is always more to learn. This book is a great place to start.

CHAPTER 1

ELEMENTS OF VISUAL STORYTELLING

In this first chapter, we will discuss a few different concepts that are necessary background information for the rest of the book. While most chapters are devoted to a single subject or area of visual storytelling, this chapter will span multiple subjects. Each concept covered in this chapter will be revisited in subsequent sections with greater detail, so if you read this chapter and are hungry for more information, don't worry . . . you will get it!

I have always said that the key to being a successful filmmaker is to understand every role of a film crew and then surround yourself with people that are better at those roles than you. I know there are many filmmakers who believe wearing every hat and having ultimate control is the only way to make a good film, but I disagree. The analogy I like to use is, "What are the chances you will be a gold medal–winning downhill skier, Grammy-winning singer, brilliant sculptor and expert marksman? About the same as you being the best writer, director, cinematographer and editor." Although the best approach is to find the most talented and skilled crew you can, you must remember that no member of a film crew works in a vacuum. Every decision we make affects the rest of the film, so we must understand what everyone else is doing in order to create the best possible film. Understanding everyone's roles will not necessarily make you an expert at every job; however, it will help you communicate with the experts with whom you are working. If you are a director, understanding cinematography, editing, producing and sound will make you a better director because you will be able to communicate your vision to the rest of the crew. As a director, being able to express your vision is crucial. That is how you truly retain control of your film. Communication with the rest of the crew is how you ensure that everyone is telling the same story; when we get down to the fundamentals, story is at the core of everything we do.

It is often said that the key to making a great film is having a great story. This is a truth that both filmmakers and audience members alike understand. But what makes a story great? Is it the characters? Is it the plot? Is it the drama or the action? The answer is *yes!* These are all components of creating a great story, but more important than any of these singular elements is how we as filmmakers tell the story, which can be told in many different ways. The most widely known is through writing. The plot and the dialogue a writer creates are the backbone of the story. These are absolutely essential for creating a great film, because without a great script, the best you can hope for is a mediocre film. I think we have all seen films with incredible special effects and breathtaking action, but we leave the theater asking ourselves, "What the hell just happened?"

While a great script is the first piece of telling a great story, it is just one of many pieces. In order to bring that story to life on the screen, we must skillfully translate those words into images. These images will make or break your film. When used correctly, a filmmaker can create a masterpiece that will be discussed for generations. When used incorrectly, a filmmaker can create confusion and boredom. The final story that we see on the screen is a fifty/fifty combination of writing and visual storytelling.

WHAT IS VISUAL STORYTELLING?

Very few audience members truly understand the art of visual storytelling on more than a superficial level, which is how we as filmmakers like it. When viewers become aware of these techniques it changes the way they watch movies, and in some ways removes just a little bit of the magic. As most filmmakers will tell you, once you know the secrets, you will never watch movies the same way. Your ability to go into "dream mode" diminishes. However, you are left with a far greater respect for the work and skill that was required to create the film.

So what is visual storytelling? Visual storytelling is how we create a mood and set a tone for the audience. It informs the audience of the theme and emotion of a scene or film. I like to think of visual storytelling as how we speak to the audience without saying a word. Visual storytelling is a language that all filmmakers speak, and most audience members understand.

I like to think of it in this way. My grandmother's first language is Spanish. When I was a child she would often speak to me in Spanish; unfortunately, I only speak English. However, based on her emotion, I could understand what she was trying to tell me. It was often the unspoken that gave me more information than her actual words. The language of visual storytelling is much the same. You may not be able to speak it, but you certainly understand it. For many of us, movies have been a big part of our lives since early childhood. The language of the cinema has been deeply infused in our subconscious, and as a result, we have a profound understanding of visual storytelling, whether we are conscious of it or not. For example, we have all seen films in the thriller or noir genre. Imagine any film of these genres where we see a detective making his way through a dark location with his gun drawn. We know something scary or dramatic is most likely going to occur. We certainly don't need our brave detective to declare, "This sure is scary!" We already know it's scary. How do we know it's scary? Well, it's a combination of visual elements that gives us that information. Adding the unnecessary dialogue is a bad use of "expositional dialogue," which we will examine later.

When it comes to visual storytelling, the first clue we often have is lighting. Lighting can instantaneously create a mood like no other element. In fact, just one frame of a well-lit scene can give the audience as much information as five pages of dialogue. If the scene has heavy contrast and shadows, that is often a clue that the filmmakers are trying to create a dramatic or intense tone. Just like in reality, heavy shadows will hide what lurks in the darkness. On the opposite end of the lighting spectrum, bright, evenly lit images are often used to create a happy or non-threatening tone.

Although these are commonly used techniques, we will spend a great deal of time discussing how to break the rules of visual storytelling to create images that are far more dynamic. One of my favorite examples is the Stanley Kubrick film *The Shining*. Kubrick decided to use bright, soft lighting for much of the film, even though it was a terrifying horror film. This use of lighting created a far more menacing world than the standard contrast-y horror lighting audiences had become accustomed to.

More often than not, the color of the light will play a part in visual storytelling as well. In fact, as a cinematographer, color of light is one of my very first considerations when I read a script. In pre-production, a great deal of time is devoted to creating a color palette for the film, which we will discuss in chapter 6. As a filmmaker, understanding the emotional effect certain colors will have on the audience is an essential skill. Red lighting, or a cold, pale, blue color can feel scary when paired with shadowy lighting, while softer whites and pastel colors have a calming effect. I often find that new filmmakers go through three distinct phases of lighting in regards to color. The first is no use of color. They simply set up their lights with no gels (colored sheets of plastic that go in front of the light to add color) or oftentimes use natural light. The next phase is when they discover colored gels. This is often an epiphany for new filmmakers and they seem to head right for what we call the "party gels." Party gels are generally bright colors that don't appear often in reality, such as red, green, pink, etc. These gels are a lot of fun but are difficult to justify in the story and often look very "stagey" or theatrical. The third and final phase is understanding how to use colored light to enhance the story. This is often accomplished through subtle use of gels and colors that appear in reality. A common technique is using color-correction gels to slightly warm up or cool down the color. This can create a mood without seeming heavy-handed.

Another important element of visual storytelling is camera movement. There are dozens of ways to move the camera and each one will elicit a different emotion within the audience. For example, a large sweeping motion from a crane might give the audience a sense of freedom and reveal the massive scale of a location, while a handheld camera movement might create a sense of intensity and danger for the audience. A director has many choices for camera movement and each one carries emotional weight. A shot as simple as two people walking down the street can be shot in dozens of ways. The director can choose to shoot this scene on a dolly, which will make the camera seem invisible and give the audience a feeling that they are following closely behind or in front of the action. The director could also choose to use a Steadicam to shoot the scene, which allows the camera to be much more mobile and often creates a more dynamic scene by allowing more camera movement. This also allows for a much more intimate scene with changing camera angles. Another possible choice for the director is handheld. The choice of handheld would create a far more dramatic scene, adding a layer of intensity and voyeurism due to the movements of the camera operator. A shaky handheld camera will add high drama and intensity to the scene, which may be the desired effect, but when used incorrectly it will make the audience instantly aware of its presence. Like all elements of film, there is a fine line between a whisper and a shout.

In addition to lighting and camera work, we will discuss other important elements of visual storytelling such as composition, framing, coverage, and story structure. Breaking down these techniques is essential to becoming a great filmmaker, but before you can apply these techniques, you must first learn whose responsibilities they are.

THE VISUAL STORYTELLING TEAM

For anyone who has watched the credits of a film, you are aware that a film crew comprises anywhere from a few crewmembers to a few dozen crewmembers, and in the case of large-budget, special effects–heavy films, hundreds of crew members. Many of these roles are reserved for larger productions and budgets; however, there are certain positions that must be present for a shoot to take place. There are three key positions that make up the core of the visual storytelling team on a film shoot. These three positions will often have support from many other crew members, but without their creative vision, it would be nearly impossible to create a visually compelling film.

DIRECTOR

The first and most well known of these is the director. When I was growing up, my dream, like many other kids, was to become a director. In fact, I told everyone who would listen that I was going to be the next big director in Hollywood. I held onto this dream until I directed my very first short film. It was at that point I swore I would never direct anything ever again. The reason was, I didn't understand the responsibilities of a director. I thought the director's role was to set up the shot, call action and then call cut, which, although partially true, is only a small portion of the job. I have found this lack of understanding of the director's responsibilities to be quite common, which leads to many misconceptions about becoming a director. As in any job, in order to become a successful director, one must understand the responsibilities involved. It is important to understand that the director will always be the creative force behind the film and have the ultimate creative say. It is the director's vision that is being created, and the entire team strives to bring that to life. While it can be said that the director wears many hats, during the production phase, he or she really has two major areas of focus.

The first is working with actors. The director is responsible for helping the actors bring their characters to life through performance. The director must make sure that their actors understand the roles they are playing and are able to create the necessary emotions. This can be overwhelming and stressful for both the director and actor. A successful director must possess many skills, including communication, patience, problem-solving and manipulation to coax strong performances from the actors. The relationship between the director and actors should be based on trust, as actors often find themselves in emotionally vulnerable situations.

The second, yet equally important responsibility of the director, is to create the visuals that will reach the screen. The director must decide what coverage will be filmed and how each shot will look. A good director will have a strong understanding of all cinematic techniques in order to create the images they need to tell their story. It is often difficult to envision how different shots will edit together, so it is necessary that directors spend a good amount of time in pre-production planning each shot. The director is the metaphorical captain of the ship, so it is important for them to be a strong leader with a clear vision. Everyone will look to the director for leadership, and in many ways, they set the tone for the production. An approachable and friendly director will often create a comfortable and laid back atmosphere, while an intense or short-tempered director will often create an environment of stress and anxiety. The job of director can be overwhelming and stressful, but it is important to remember that they are not working alone. They have support from an entire crew and should utilize them accordingly.

CINEMATOGRAPHER

The next essential member of the team is the cinematographer. Although almost everyone is familiar, at least partially, with the director, very few people really know what a cinematographer does, and as far as most cinematographers are concerned, that is a good thing. Cinematography is something that to a general viewing audience should be invisible. So what is this mysterious thing called cinematography? Simply put, cinematography is the art of lighting and camera movement for the cinema. But that clinical definition does not do it justice. A more accurate definition is "a cinematographer uses lights and camera to create the world the characters inhabit and the emotions they feel." Cinematography is one of the major components of visual storytelling, and without great cinematography, you are really only telling half the story.

If you still don't understand what cinematography is, perhaps this will help. Many years back I was at an event with many well-known filmmakers. A film student approached a cinematographer with whom I was speaking and asked, "What exactly is a cinematographer's job?" Given the stature of this cinematographer, I was expecting to hear an overly inflated egomaniacal response; however, what I heard has shaped my definition of cinematography and, in many ways, my career. This cinematographer responded with, "My responsibility is to bring the director's vision to life. No more, no less."

This philosophy is what is at the core of every great director/cinematographer relationship. Often, directors do not communicate their vision in a tangible description. They, instead, use emotions to describe the scene they hope to create. For example, I have had many directors say to me, "I want this scene to feel scary, or happy, or peaceful." It is the cinematographer's job to take that emotion and turn it into something tangible. The tools we use to bring these emotions to life are lights, cameras and lenses. There is a great deal of interpretation in this translation, so nailing the look the director is envisioning is not always easy. It takes time to form this line of communication and learn each other's style. This is why when a director and cinematographer form a strong relationship you will often see multiple collaborations between the two. Such is the case with Steven Spielberg and Janusz Kaminski, the Coen brothers and Roger Deakins, and Quentin Tarantino and Robert Richardson.

Although this type of communication is the case with many director/cinematographer relationships, it is not always the norm. Many directors are very specific with the look they are trying to create and have an extremely strong understanding of cinemaphotographic technique. This can often leave little room for interpretation for a cinematographer and in many cases renders the cinematographer a technician instead of an artist. Each director/cinematographer relationship will be different, but it is important to understand that the director together with the cinematographer are at the heart of all things creative. I like to think of them as the pitcher and catcher on a baseball team. Although there are many people on the field, those are the two most important roles. Ultimately, this pair of creative minds is responsible for producing the images that end up on the screen.

PRODUCTION DESIGNER

The third key player in the visual storytelling team is the production designer. For some odd reason, the production designer gets the least recognition out of the three key members of the visual storytelling team. But anyone who works in the film industry knows that without a talented and dedicated production designer, the director and cinematographer will be severely limited. If the cinematographer is responsible for creating the film's world using lights and camera, the production designer is responsible for creating the physical world using sets, paint, furniture, props, etc. Their work helps to create a tone for the film and—along with the director and cinematographer—the production designer creates a color palette and style for the film. This work begins in pre-production and once the sets and style are discussed, the production designer begins the painstaking job of creating detailed sketches of each set. These sketches will depict, in great detail, the sets that will be created, or if the set is an existing location, how it will be changed to fit the film. Once these sketches are completed, the production designer along with the rest of the art department will begin building these sets. Here's the easiest way to understand the importance of a production designer. Imagine you are shooting a film that takes place inside of a thirteenth-century castle. You, however, are shooting the film on a sound stage. Without the production designer, your set will be an empty room with no beautiful stone fireplaces, no massive dining rooms and certainly no candlelit chandeliers. Just an empty room with white walls and wooden floors. Far too often, new filmmakers forgo a production designer because they are shooting on location and just use the items on the set. This is a huge mistake. Just like all other visual elements, the production design and props should help to define the characters. A good production designer understands the characters and surrounds them with elements that represent them.

GIVING THE AUDIENCE ENOUGH INFORMATION

Perhaps the most common mistake I see new filmmakers commit is not giving the audience enough information up front. Audience members need basic information in order to connect with the characters and the earlier this connection can be made, the better. Information can come in many forms, including dialogue and visual information, but without it, the audience can't connect with the characters or story. Filmmakers often assume that because they know the story, the audience will as well. This is certainly not the case. While a writer has spent months, maybe even years, getting to know their characters, the audience knows nothing. Characters, in many ways, become an extension of the writer, but to an uninformed audience, they are complete strangers. The first moments of a film are the cinematic equivalent of a blind date. So how do we give the audience what they need? It's simple . . . show them! Within the first few moments of your film use visuals to communicate the pertinent information. What information is pertinent? Well, that, of course, depends on the film you are making. But in most cases, we, at the very least, need to get to know our protagonist and genre. This information will allow us to continue on our journey. It is also important to understand how much time you have to communicate this information. In a feature length film, you often have twenty to thirty minutes, but in a short film you might have as little as thirty seconds. This is why it's important to create visuals with the maximum amount of impact. Much of this can be done in the "opening image." The opening image is the first image or scene we see on screen. I cannot stress enough the importance of a strong opening image. Let me give you two scenarios as examples.

OPENING IMAGE 1:

A man is sitting on a couch, alone, in a white-walled apartment, wearing jeans and a white T-shirt.

Questions:
Who is this man?
What type of person is he?
What is the genre of our film?
What do we know about him?

Answer:
I have no idea!

Why? Because we have given the audience no information. This is what I like to call the "some-guy syndrome." Some-guy syndrome is when we introduce the audience to just some guy. This type of opening image does nothing to inform the audience or move the story along. It is wasted time, and in a film, every shot matters. There are no throwaway shots in a film; every frame should support your story and give the audience visual information.

Think of a movie like a photography exhibit. Imagine going to a gallery and every third photograph is beautiful, while every photo in between is out of focus and underexposed. That would be a disappointing exhibit. The same is true with a film. If some of your shots are well composed and provide information while others are wasted frames, that isn't a rewarding or successful film.

Let's look at another scenario for an opening image.

OPENING IMAGE 2:

A man is standing in front of a burning building wearing a yellow jacket and pants, a red helmet, and carrying an axe. The building suddenly explodes, and the man runs into the fire. He soon emerges from the flames holding a child.

Questions:

Who is this man?

What type of person is he?

What is the genre of our film?

What do we know about him?

Answer:

I think you get my point. The characters from the two scenarios might be the exact same character and eventually you might get around to giving the audience the same information, but clearly, the second scenario is far more compelling. Obviously, not all characters warrant a hero's introduction, but that does not mean you can't introduce them in the midst of a compelling action that helps to visually define them.

The more visual information we can give the audience, the more connected they will feel to the characters and the story. I like to think of a good opening image like baggage in a relationship. We will carry it with us for the duration of the film, and it will continue to guide and inform our feelings about the characters. You only get one shot at a first impression, so be sure to create a lasting and effective one.

EXPOSITION: IMAGES VS. DIALOGUE

Exposition is "the exposing of information about characters, or story." As a filmmaker, you have the option of using either dialogue or images to tell your story, which can be a difficult decision to make. This frequently leads filmmakers to use dialogue because it's often easier than creating compelling images. Any good story will be told through a combination of visuals and dialogue, but knowing when to use each element is vital. My personal philosophy is use dialogue only when you can't express your message through images.

Using dialogue to give the audience information is called expositional dialogue and is a necessary part of telling a story. However, when used incorrectly, expositional dialogue can feel heavy-handed and "cheesy." Let's go back to our firefighter example. That exact same scenario could have been told through dialogue. Remember the guy in blue jeans and a T-shirt sitting on his couch? Well, imagine he picks up the phone and places a call and says, "Mom, you're never going to guess what happened to me last night. I was working as a firefighter and I responded to a call. When I got there the house was engulfed in flames and I ran inside and saved a child. I'm a hero now."

Now in both scenarios we have the exact same information, but which would be more pleasing to the audience, the visuals of our hero saving a child from a burning building or the dialogue of him recounting this story to his mom? That's right, the visuals. So how do we know which to use? Well, it's fairly simple. Just ask yourself, "Would it be more effective to show it or say it?" I am in no way implying that using dialogue for exposition is a bad thing. However, it must be used sparingly.

Of course, visual storytelling is made up of a lot more than just opening images; otherwise, our films would only be ten seconds long. Every frame of our movie is telling a story, and every inch of every frame as well. The question you must ask yourself is, "Is this frame telling my story?" Always remember; if the information contained within these frames isn't helping your story, it is hurting it. As we move through the chapters of this book, the concepts of visual storytelling will become clearer and theories will give way to techniques. If you find yourself feeling slightly overwhelmed, don't panic, that is a good sign. It means you are beginning to understand the massive array of possibilities.

CHAPTER 2

BASIC STORY STRUCTURE

As any filmmaker knows, a great script is a solid beginning to creating a great film. And in order to write a great script, you must understand basic story structure. Even the best ideas for scripts can fall flat when story structure is not followed. I am not suggesting that there is only one formula for writing a script, but understanding the progression of a story is crucial.

Although this book is not designed to turn you into a screenwriter, there are certain elements that all directors and cinematographers must understand in order to tell their story visually. Without this knowledge, it is extremely difficult to tell a story fully. One of the most common pitfalls I see with new filmmakers is a lack of attention to the first act of their film, which is why we will spend the majority of this chapter focused on that. What some filmmakers don't seem to understand is that without a strong first act, no one cares about the second act. But, before we get too caught up in fine details, let's go back to the beginning.

Let's begin with some basic terminology that many of you are probably already familiar with. I'll include some of the misconceptions about the nuances of these concepts.

PROTAGONIST

There is often confusion about what a protagonist is. Over the years, I have heard many people describe the protagonist as "the hero" or the "good guy," but that is not a requirement. In fact, there are many wonderful films in which the protagonist is a bad person or a person who has done something terribly wrong. The main guideline when creating a protagonist is simply that they are the character whose journey we follow. It is their story. A close friend of mine, a talented professor and screenwriter, uses the definition, "The protagonist is the character that drives the action." She likes this definition because it implies that the protagonist must be "active." You are probably wondering what I mean by "active protagonist," so let's break it down.

ACTIVE VS. PASSIVE PROTAGONIST

An active protagonist is a character who actively pursues what he or she wants. A *passive* protagonist is a character who waits for what they want to come to them. We as audience members don't like passive protagonists. They seem lazy and undeserving of reward. For example, let's say we are writing a script about a man who needs fifty thousand dollars to save his family's home.

In Scenario A (active protagonist) our protagonist works day and night to earn the money he needs, sacrificing his own well-being and is finally able to save enough money to help his family.

In Scenario B (passive protagonist) our protagonist is frustrated that he can't afford to save his family's home, so he goes to the store and buys some beer. While there, he buys a lottery ticket and wins fifty thousand dollars. He takes the money and saves his family's home. Both films have the same outcome, but which would be more rewarding to watch? That's right, the active protagonist. When in doubt, make your protagonist active! Decide what the character wants and have them actively pursue it.

Another important rule to remember is that there will generally be only one protagonist per movie. We like to follow one person and their perspective, so multiple protagonists can confuse an audience. There are a few exceptions, the most common being scripts with multiple storylines, meaning there is more than one story happening within the film. With scripts like that, there is often a protagonist for each storyline.

Another important thing to remember with protagonists is ensuring that the audience connects with them. This is especially true when creating a protagonist who does bad things. For example, any protagonist that is an anti-hero or criminal can be difficult for the audience to relate to. It is your job as the filmmaker to humanize the character. This can be as simple as a moment of kindness or as complicated as an entire scene giving backstory. We will revisit this concept in a few pages.

ANTAGONIST

Just like with protagonists, there is often some confusion about antagonists in films. The common misconception is that the antagonist is "the bad guy," but again, that is not necessarily the case. In any good heist film, the police are generally the antagonists, even though they are doing the right thing. So how do you define the antagonist? The antagonist is the character that opposes the protagonist. They simply want the opposite of what the protagonist wants.

Antagonists come in many different forms. The first and most common is what is often referred to as person vs. person. This is your common Batman vs. Joker or Luke Skywalker vs. Darth Vader scenario. But you can also have person vs. group. Think someone trying to escape zombies. The group of zombies is now the antagonist. Another option is person vs. self. In a person vs. self story, the protagonist is battling against him/herself. Common themes are mental illness or physical disabilities.

In some films, antagonists aren't even people. One example is person vs. nature. These types of antagonists are often dangerous weather such as storms or floods or natural disasters such as earthquakes or fires. Wild animals can also be antagonists and fall into the person vs. nature category as well. Remember, all a character or circumstance needs to be an antagonist is to prevent the protagonist from getting what they want.

DRAMATIC IRONY

When the audience knows something the characters don't, that's dramatic irony. For example, if we see a shot of a bomb in the trunk of a car, but the person driving the car is unaware that the bomb is there, that is dramatic irony. This technique is very useful for building tension amongst the audience. Perhaps the greatest practitioner ever of dramatic irony was Alfred Hitchcock. It was this technique that garnered him the title "The Master of Suspense." If you've ever had the feeling when watching a movie that you wanted to yell some piece of information to the characters, such as, "The killer is hiding behind the door!" then you are familiar with dramatic irony.

VISUAL NARRATIVE

Telling the story through visuals rather than dialogue is visual narrative. Often filmmakers will create a visual narrative sequence to give the audience information in a more eloquent way than having the characters say it. It's a great way of forming connections to characters or giving backstory.

So now that we are familiar with some of the terminology and concepts, let's get into the meat of telling a story.

THREE-ACT STRUCTURE

Films are generally made up of three distinct and separate acts. Each one of these acts is essential to telling a complete story, and when one of these acts is missing, the audience will often feel unsatisfied. Each act fulfills a different goal and the combination of the three acts is what creates a complete film. Just like any other rule, there are of course exceptions, but the majority of films will follow this structure.

FIRST ACT

The goal of the first act is to set up the story and introduce the characters. The first act is absolutely essential to the progression of the story. However, I often find that it is the one element that new filmmakers spend the least amount of time crafting. The first act is not the most exciting act, which is probably why it tends to get ignored, but it is perhaps the most important of the three acts. The first act is where we meet the protagonist and gather information

about them. It is where we find out a character's hopes and wants and generally what makes them tick. What makes the first act so important is this is where the audience forms a connection and a bond with your protagonist. It is also where we are first introduced to the main conflict in the story.

Earlier I mentioned the importance of the first act when you create a protagonist that commits bad deeds. Let's elaborate. If your protagonist commits a murder in the second act, the audience is far more likely to forgive them and justify it if we have formed a bond with them in the first act. We must find a way of making even the most despicable protagonists human and the first act is often our opportunity to do so. Although not all protagonists will be flawed or criminal, the significance of the first act remains. If the audience doesn't feel connected to the protagonist, they won't be interested in going along on their journey.

It's no fun to watch a story about a character whom we know nothing about, so it is up to the writer and director to give as much information as possible. Too often films suffer from a lack of information. Directors often assume because they know so much about the character the audience will as well. This is certainly not the case. Your protagonist is a complete stranger to the audience; all they know is what you show them. When writing your script, or directing your film, ask yourself, "How much about this character does the audience really know?" Then find ways of giving even more information

So, how do we give the audience visual information? Let's start at the beginning. How you open your movie is absolutely essential!

OPENING IMAGE

The opening image of your film is the first thing your audience will see. It is important that it carries some weight and information. It is not just an arbitrary image. First impressions are almost impossible to get rid of, and this is where the audience's first impression is formed. Use that! Create an opening image that gives the audience information about your character. In a feature length film, you have the luxury of taking roughly thirty minutes to introduce your protagonist, but in a short film, you might have as little as thirty seconds.

Although your protagonist doesn't have to be the first thing the audience sees on screen, I have found that, especially in short films, it is best for the protagonist to be the first person the audience sees. As always, there are exceptions to this suggestion, but it's a good place to start. Audience members are hungry for information, so, often they will try to connect with the first person they see. That can be dangerous if the first person they see isn't the protagonist.

In chapter 1, we discussed what I call the "some-guy syndrome," so be sure to introduce your characters in the midst of an action

that defines them. It is fine to show the audience a character doing nothing, but remember, the audience will use that to define them. You can also use dialogue to give the audience information about your protagonist, but as we discussed previously, images almost always work better.

If you start your second act without having given your audience enough information, they won't be connected to your character. Make the audience feel a connection with your protagonist. There should be something interesting or likeable about this character. Likeable doesn't necessarily mean they are warm and kindhearted; it simply means we have to like watching them. The character should possess some quality that makes them fascinating to the audience. No one wants to watch a film about a person who is boring.

Not only do you need to introduce your protagonist in the first act, you also need to introduce the story. The easiest way of doing this is to set up the character's world. Most films will start by showing us the life of their protagonist. This makes the audience comfortable and allows them to bond with the character.

To illustrate this, let's create a story. I will use an example I often use in my classes—me! Here are a few bits of information about me that we can use to craft our story. I am a husband, a father of two daughters and a college professor. I love my family, my life and my career. Now let's take that information and create a ridiculous story, starting with our first act. I like to think of a film as a train traveling down railroad tracks from point A to point B, so let's start at the beginning. We can open our film with our protagonist (me) on the phone telling someone all of the information I have just given you, but that wouldn't be very cinematic, so let's show the audience this information.

The film opens with me and my wife asleep in bed. Our two daughters and fluffy dog come running in and jump on the bed, waking us up. The next scene is all of us eating breakfast together and having a wonderful morning. Next, I am dressed and leaving for work. I kiss my family goodbye and exit. I then arrive at work and teach my class. From my demeanor and disposition, it is clear that I love my job and enjoy interacting with my students.

This short opening sequence has just given the audience a wealth of information, but more importantly it has helped them connect with the protagonist. One of the most important pieces of information we have given the audience is the protagonist's "want." The want is pretty straightforward; it is simply what the protagonist desires. In our story the protagonist wants to live a happy life and grow old with his family. This want is what will drive the protagonist when things don't go according to plan. We have now created a successful opening sequence using "visual narrative." Had we chosen to give this same information through dialogue, it would have been far less rewarding and there would be very little emotional connection.

So, our train (story) has left the station and is now traveling down the railroad tracks; Destination, happily ever after. Of course in any good film, it can't be that simple. Something has to go wrong. That something is called the inciting incident.

INCITING INCIDENT

In the first act the character is going about their daily business, which, if done correctly, is giving the audience backstory and information. This may be mundane, this may be exciting, but it is the path the character is on. Suddenly, a giant boulder falls right on our railroad tracks, forcing us to hit the track switcher and go in a different direction. This boulder is the inciting incident. It is an impassible roadblock on our journey to happily ever after. Let's revisit our story and insert an inciting incident.

After our protagonist finishes teaching his class, he hops in his car and heads home, excited to see his family. When he arrives home, there is a giant crowd of spectators and news crews gathered outside of his house. He frantically runs to the front door but is stopped by police, who then inform him that his family has been abducted by aliens.

This is the inciting incident. It is a giant roadblock stopping him from getting what he wants and forcing him to go in a different direction. Although we are getting close to the second act, we are not quite there yet. After the inciting incident, there is one more important piece of business to attend to. The protagonist must make a decision about what to do. This is called the "lock-in." This is the point where you decide if your character is going to be an active protagonist or a passive protagonist. Let's insert the lock into our story.

Our protagonist's family has been abducted by aliens, and he must decide what he's going to do about it. He can sit on his front porch and wait for the aliens to bring his family back (passive protagonist) or he can build a spaceship and go get his family back (active protagonist).

SECOND ACT

If I had to sum up the second act in one word it would be *journey*. The second act is almost always the longest of the three acts. In fact, it's generally the same length as the first and third acts combined. The second act is where all of the exciting things happen, which is why so many new filmmakers accidently skip the first act and start their film in the second act. The problem with that is the audience will have no idea what is going on, nor will they care, because the characters are complete strangers.

Each semester I assign my students film projects to shoot. There is one project that has always stuck with me, and it is a perfect example of what happens when you skip an act. Their film opens with two men dressed in black military clothes and ski masks holding M16 rifles, standing on the front porch of a house at night. All of a sudden, they kick in the front door and run inside the house. They tie everyone up inside and steal a briefcase from the table. The gunmen then run out the door and the film ends. I remember thinking to myself, "Wow, that film looked great. I wish I knew what it was about!"

I had no idea what the story was about, I had no idea who the protagonist was, I had no idea who the antagonist was and, frankly, I didn't really care. The reason? There was absolutely no first act. We had no information about the story or characters; therefore, as exciting as it was, we weren't emotionally invested. Had this film had a first act explaining the story and introducing the characters, perhaps we could have formed a connection, but because any background information was nonexistent, there was no connection. Always remember, the success of your second act hinges on your first act.

So what elements do we need in a second act? Again, this isn't a screenwriting book, so I'm going to stick to the essentials. The first and most important element of a second act is conflict. This conflict should increase as the story progresses through the second act. The protagonist must meet obstacles along the way that create this conflict.

Let's go back to our story and add some conflict. At the end of the first act our protagonist decided to build a spaceship; the problem, he has no idea how to build a spaceship. This is the first obstacle and source of conflict. Each additional source of conflict must be bigger than the previous obstacle. This is called "rising conflict." Along with conflict comes another important element, "stakes." Something must always be at stake for your protagonist and conflict should interfere with that. For example, what is at stake in our story is the protagonist's family, so all forms of conflict should challenge that. Someone trashing the protagonist's house, although discouraging, does nothing to interfere with his mission. However, building a spaceship to rescue his family and having someone destroy that, does. Always ask yourself, "What is at stake when creating conflict and obstacles?" If your obstacle doesn't challenge what's at stake, it isn't an effective obstacle. Since I can't build a spaceship, I decide to kidnap a scientist who can. This leads to the police chasing us: more conflict!

Next comes the midpoint or first culmination. This is where the protagonist finally has a breakthrough and sees some success. This is generally followed by more conflict. In our story this is where the scientist listens to the protagonist and agrees to help. They work together to build the spaceship only to discover it doesn't fly. Finally, after a breakthrough, they are able to make the spaceship work and they head into space.

This leads us to the main culmination of the film. This is where our protagonist must land on a strange planet and attempt to rescue his family. Again, the second act is often the most exciting and is the meat of the journey.

THIRD ACT

The third act of a film is all about the resolution. This is where you tell the audience how the character has changed, what will become of them, and whether or not they got what they wanted.

But before you can get to the resolution, you must have a climax. The climax is the most exciting point in the film and everything is at stake for your protagonist.

In our story, this is the point where he must fight the aliens and rescue his family.

Next comes the character arc, which is how we show the change a character has experienced throughout the film. This does not mean your character has to be changed for the better; it just means they should be different than they were in the beginning of the film. They can start as a good guy and end as a bad guy, they can start as a bad guy and end as a good guy, or they can start as a bad guy and end as a bad guy, as long as they are somehow changed as a result of their experience.

The best character arcs show how the character is changed as a direct result of what they have learned on their journey. It is always best to begin setting this up in the first act. This can be done in many ways, but one of my favorite techniques is to use a character flaw. Setting up a character flaw in the first act and showing a change in the third act is extremely rewarding. One of my favorite examples of this is in the *Back to the Future* trilogy. In parts two and three, they establish that Marty's character flaw is that he won't back down when called a chicken. It gets him into serious trouble many times, but at the end of part three, we see that he has learned from those mistakes and no longer reacts to name calling.

In our story, when our protagonist returns to Earth with his family he realizes he has a new found love for space and adventure and is bored by his old life. He and his family decide to travel through space exploring distant galaxies rather than live on Earth. It could easily be set up in the first act that our protagonist is a homebody and doesn't like adventure or danger. This would show a dramatic change in our character and would be very rewarding for the audience.

This leads to our resolution, which is simply the end of the film. It shows the audience how the characters have changed and who they are now.

In our story, it is a simple scene of our protagonist and his family flying through space, smiling.

Although this may seem complicated, I have simplified this structure as much as possible. There are far more story elements and milestones, but for our purposes of creating a well-rounded story this should suffice. Now that you understand the basics of three-act structure, let's talk about what you need to craft a complete story.

SIX STEPS OF BASIC STORY STRUCTURE

There is a guide I like to use when writing or reading any script that helps me identify missing elements. It is essentially a bite-size summary of everything we just covered. There are six key elements that I like to focus on. Of course there are many more than six elements that make up a story, but for simplicity, we will focus on these six. When these six steps are followed, you will almost always create a complete story. Making it a great story is up to you.

Character: Every film is about a character. This character is the protagonist and without one you have no story. They must be developed in the first act and you must give the audience ample information about your character. Make them interesting or likeable and make them a person, not a caricature.

Want: Almost every movie you've ever seen is about a character who wants something. Your character must desperately want something and be willing to sacrifice everything to get it! This want should be the most important thing in the world to your protagonist. This want can be something physical, emotional, spiritual, or other, but without it, there is no journey. The want should also be established in the first act.

Action: Your character must take action to get what he wants. If there is one thing the audience can't stand it's a passive protagonist. This is when the protagonist does nothing to get what he wants, but rather waits for his want to come to him. The action can be anything from a large physical journey to a small emotional journey. This action will continue throughout the entire film but will be central in the second act. The second act is all about the action.

Conflict: A film wouldn't be very exciting if your character wants something and then gets it. The protagonist should meet with some sort of conflict. This conflict should be overwhelming and a direct result of the action a character has taken to get what they want. Conflicts can be any type of difficulty: hardship, challenge or roadblock. Conflict will also primarily live in the second act. There should be multiple forms of conflict, each one more daunting than the last. Be sure to remember the "stakes" when creating conflict. If the conflict doesn't jeopardize the stakes, it isn't effective conflict.

Climax: The climax is the most exciting point in the film. This is where the protagonist must make a final decision and is forced to risk it all or die trying. The climax comes in the third act.

Resolution: As we discussed before, the resolution is where the audience finds out what happened to the characters and how the protagonist is changed. We will also find out if the protagonist succeeded or failed in obtaining their goal. The key to creating a great ending is to make it something that the audience didn't see coming, yet is perfectly logical. This can be extremely difficult, but one great approach is to combine the audience's hopes and fears to create your ending.

CREATING A CHARACTER

As we discussed, creating a character that people can connect with is absolutely essential. Try to get away from telling the audience about your character. Rather, show the audience what they need to know. One of the best approaches for creating characters is to create a mini-biography for them. Once you understand your characters you can easily decide how to visually portray them. Here are some elements to consider:

1. **Social Role**: What is their job or primary relationship? What role do they play in society? Is your character a banker, a mother, a hot dog vendor, a homeless man, a drug addict, etc?

2. **Specific Hobby/Interest:** Give your character a specific hobby or interest; consider what they love to do most in the world. Why?

Because people who are passionate about something are more interesting to watch.

3. Heartfelt Desire: What do they desire most in the world? True love? Connection? Power?

4. Deepest Fear: What do they fear most in the world? Public speaking? Being stuck in an elevator? Romantic relationships?

Next, define and describe your protagonist emotionally. Who is your main character? You'll want to use specific adjectives: shy, insecure, lonely, agoraphobic, under-appreciated, over-worked, etc. The goal is for you to understand them on an emotional level.

Now that you have developed your characters on the inside, you can begin to develop them on the outside. You need to decide how to visually represent your characters. This will give the audience more information than you can imagine, so think carefully when developing. Here are some visual ways to convey who your character is:

Physical Appearance: How do they look; their hair, makeup and overall appearance? What are they wearing? Are they dirty or materialistic? A punk rocker or a banker?

2. Environment/Surroundings: Where are they? In a dark and dirty alley? On a rooftop watching a sunset?

3. Props/Activities: How we first meet your characters will affect how we relate to them for the duration of your film. What are your characters doing when we first meet them? Sharpening a knife? Helping a stray animal? Binge drinking?

4. Action/Inaction/Reaction: What they do—or don't do—or how they respond will convey an immense amount of information about their character.

Often these visual elements will be the first clues the audience has as to who your characters are; be sure to take them seriously. Early in the story, audience members will try and use every detail to define and understand characters, so everything we see should help tell your story. If it doesn't, it's hurting your story.

It's important to understand that the audience knows nothing about a character when the movie begins. Really, all we have to go on are stereotypes. If you show the audience a guy in a leather vest, covered in tattoos, smoking a cigarette and riding a motorcycle, the audience is never going to say "that must be a priest." It may very well be a priest but the audience will never make that leap. I'm all for breaking stereotypes on screen, but it's also important to understand how to do it. It's a simple and silent way of informing the audience. Always remember, the audience needs more information than you think. The more you develop your characters, the more emotionally connected your audience will be.

CHAPTER 3

COMPOSITION

Now that we have covered what it takes to craft a story, we can begin to discuss how we bring that story to life, visually. This will be our first journey into the language of visuals and hopefully bridge the gap between script and screen. Although a great amount of information can be disseminated during the writing process, images can carry far more weight than words, and if the filmmaker has done their job, the audience will know exactly how they are supposed to feel without a need for expositional dialogue. Images work on a visceral level; in fact, we often aren't even conscious of our emotions; they are simply a reflex.

Few of us really know why we are feeling what we feel. After this chapter, you will. **Spoiler Alert!** You will never again watch movies the same way. Once you become aware of the techniques filmmakers use, you will be much more cognizant of them, making it far more difficult for you as an audience member to enter what I call "dreamland." This is the state where you are no longer focused on reality but rather fully engrossed in the film. The better a filmmaker you become, the harder it will be for you to tune out your inner director. It happens to us all, but in exchange, we are left with an even greater experience. The experience of understanding the process a filmmaker went through to create their vision and a respect for the work they have created.

Now that we've gotten our warning out of the way, let's proceed.

In the first chapter, I alluded to the significance of creating dynamic and powerful images and that everything in your frame must help to tell your story. I once had a professor in film school tell me, "The audience will live and die in your rectangle." To which I replied, "Huh?" He went on to explain that the audience has no information other than what you show them in your frame (rectangle), so if you are expecting them to know something you haven't shown them, think again. So how do we ensure that the frames we create are communicating the correct information?

The first step is to have a strong understanding of composition. For those of you who are unaware, composition is the placement or arrangements of elements in a work of art. Notice I said, "a work of art," rather than, "a film." That's because all art forms have some type of composition. There is a reason Mozart is known as a "composer." He is taking all of the elements (musical notes) and creating a piece of art (a composition).

We could spend chapters discussing composition in other forms of art, but for now, let's stick to composition as it pertains to film. Some of the most common elements of composition in film are placement of actors, placement of camera, camera height, headroom, and looking room, but there are many more. We will cover quite a few in this chapter, but before we do, I want to make one thing very clear. There are many "rules" of composition, all of which have a place, but what is essential for you as a filmmaker to understand is that not only can you break these rules, I implore you to do so! However, just like anything else, you must understand the rules in order to break them with purpose. Following these rules will give the audience the necessary information, but breaking them with purpose will create a deeper and more meaningful experience. It is the breaking of these film conventions that often creates films that are celebrated for a lifetime.

Before we begin making bold and powerful visual statements, we must first simply understand how to compose our frames. The majority of your scenes don't call for groundbreaking composition; in fact, the best approach is often to try and keep your composition invisible, so simply creating a balanced and well-composed frame will allow the audience to become engrossed in the story. There is a basic template that we use to ensure we are composing our frames correctly.

THE RULE OF THIRDS

In order to understand where to place objects in the frame, you first have to understand how to visualize the frame. We use a very simple technique called "The Rule of Thirds." The Rule of Thirds is a grid that divides the frame into nine small boxes. Think of it like a tic tac toe board. From now on, every time you frame a shot superimpose this image over your frame. This will tell you exactly where to place objects and people.

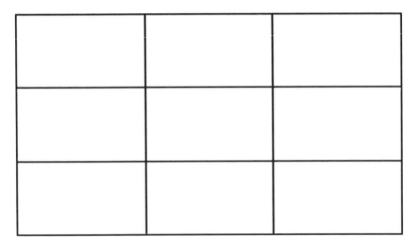

FIG. 3.1. THE RULE OF THIRDS GRID.

FIG. 3.2. IMPORTANT OBJECTS LAND IN THE INTERSECTIONS OF THE GRID.

This rule is actually quite simple. Important elements belong in one of the four intersecting points. It doesn't have to be spot on, but it should be close.

Objects will rarely be placed in the center of the frame, although there are exceptions, which we will discuss shortly. The reason is that audience members like to examine a frame and gather information. When important objects are centered, you are basically force-feeding information to your audience rather than creating a subtle hint and allowing audience members to search.

One of the most basic applications of the Rule of Thirds is for giving characters the correct amount of headroom. Headroom

is the amount of room from the top of the head to the top of the frame. Although it may seem arbitrary, it is anything but. In fact, there is an exact science to figuring out how much headroom a subject should have. A surefire way to reveal yourself as a new filmmaker is to make amateur mistakes like incorrect headroom. Using the Rule of Thirds to determine headroom is as simple as intersecting the actor's eyes with the top horizontal line in the Rule of Thirds grid. Simply put, the eyes go in the top third.

From the widest shot to the tightest shot, this will keep your actors framed correctly with the perfect amount of headroom. One thing you will notice as you move from wider shots to tighter shots is that the amount of headroom will decrease significantly.

FIG. 3.3. CORRECT HEADROOM.

FIG. 3.5. GIVING THE ACTOR A HAIRCUT.

FIG. 3.4. INCORRECT HEADROOM.

Eventually, you will even begin to cut off the top of the actor's head. Don't worry, that is normal, so normal we even have a name for it. It's called "giving the actor a haircut."

This very simple and basic rule is one that is always followed . . . almost.

Earlier, I mentioned the significance of breaking the rules of composition, and this rule is certainly meant to be broken. Too much headroom makes a person look insignificant or weak. This can be used to your advantage. If your character is in a situation where they have lost their power, or are feeling insignificant, you can give them more headroom. Often you will see subjects placed in the lower third of the frame to accomplish this effect. It can also

FIG. 3.6. A LOT OF HEADROOM REVEALS THE SCALE OF THE LOCATION.

FIG. 3.7. ASYMMETRICAL COMPOSITION: PLACING THE SUBJECT IN AN INTERSECTING POINT OF THE GRID.

be used to show the massive scale of a character's surroundings, as though a location or situation is enveloping them.

However, you must use caution. Giving a character too much headroom accidently can make the audience feel as though something is going to enter the frame and occupy that space, which can be very distracting. When framing your shot just remind yourself of the Rule of Thirds. After a while it will become second nature.

SYMMETRY

Although it is common practice to create asymmetrical frames by placing objects of significance in one of the four intersection points, this is not the only approach.

Many filmmakers prefer to forgo this technique and create symmetrical frames. A symmetrical frame is one that is balanced, often centering the subject or point of interest with matching objects on each side. This technique is considered un-cinematic by some because it creates a more theatrical or "stagey" feel, but for many filmmakers, this is the preferred method. In fact, some of the greatest filmmakers, including Stanley Kubrick, Wes Anderson, and the Coen brothers, often employ this technique quite successfully. Although centering a person in the frame breaks with typical film conventions, it can be a powerful tool. Symmetrical frames force the audience to look at a particular point, avoiding distractions. This can be effective during emotional moments in your film, or when you need the audience to focus on one point of the frame. Centering a person during a close-up or medium

FIG. 3.8. SYMMETRICAL COMPOSITION: CENTERING THE SUBJECT.

FIG. 3.9. SYMMETRICAL COMPOSITION.

close-up will draw the audience's attention directly to the subject's emotional state. Although the subject is in the center of the frame, the eyes are still intersecting with the top third to maintain the correct amount of headroom.

Symmetrical frames are also very pleasing to the eye. They create a passive and comfortable sensation amongst the audience. Although some directors choose to use symmetrical images through the entire film, others use it only for certain scenes. Whatever type of composition you choose to create, do so with purpose. Remember that every decision you make will carry emotional weight.

FIG. 3.10. SYMMETRICAL COMPOSITION.

LEADING ROOM AND LOOKING ROOM

Another rule of composition involving the Rule of Thirds is "leading room." Imagine a character is walking from the right side of the screen to the left, and we are looking at them in profile. The amount or room in front of and behind your subject is important. The general rule is to place the subject's back intersecting with the back vertical line using the Rule of Thirds. This means there will be substantially more room in front of the subject than behind them.

This feels comfortable to an audience because we know there is no imminent danger in front of them and no room for someone to sneak up behind them. Just like the correct amount of headroom, it just feels "right." The goal is not to create a mesmerizing frame,

but rather to make the camera invisible. Of course, like all rules of composition, this one can be broken as well. Moving a subject to the front of the frame with a lot of room behind them is a trick often used in horror and thriller films to make the audience feel uneasy. It hides what is directly in front of the person, making us feel like there is danger just on the other side of the frame and also creates a large open space behind the subject for someone to sneak up on the character. Placing a subject toward the edge of the frame can also create the feeling of imprisonment. It makes the audience feel as though your character is trapped, not just physically, but also emotionally. For example, if a character is put in a situation he or she is not comfortable with but has no escape, placing their face closer to the edge of the frame will create an emotion for the audience that mimics the situation.

FIG. 3.11. LEADING ROOM MAKES THE AUDIENCE COMFORTABLE.

FIG. 3.12. LACK OF LEADING ROOM MAKES THE AUDIENCE UNEASY.

FIG. 3.13. LOOKING ROOM FEELS NATURAL.

FIG. 3.14. LACK OF LEADING ROOM CREATES A CLAUSTROPHOBIC FEELING.

As you get closer to a person's face, the same rules apply, only the term is referred to as "looking room," or "nose room."

Similar to leading room, the back of the character's head will be moved toward the back vertical line in the Rule of Thirds grid. Again, this makes the audience feel comfortable that there is no imminent danger in front of or behind the subject. The same rules apply when it comes to breaking this.

Just like in wider shots, crowding a character's face in the corner of the frame will either give the appearance that a character is trapped or in danger. In fact, it can often be more impactful than with a wider shot because we are closer to the subject's face which

also maximizes emotion. This can be a handy trick when trying to build suspense in a scene.

EYES

The next rule is perhaps the most important we will discuss in this chapter.

In order for us to connect with your characters on an emotional level, we must be able to see their eyes. In reality, the more we look into a person's eyes the more connected we will become to them. The same concept applies in film. The old expression "the

FIG. 3.15. PROFILE CREATES A DISCONNECT BETWEEN THE AUDIENCE AND THE SUBJECT.

FIG. 3.16. FILMING CLOSER TO THE EYE LINE CREATES A STRONGER CONNECTION.

eyes are the window to the soul" is absolutely true on screen. If you film your character in profile or hide their eyes behind sunglasses, the chance of the audience forming a connection with them is minimal. However, if you show the audience your character's eyes, the audience will often form a stronger connection to them.

Creating a disconnect can also be an effective technique. If you don't want the audience to connect with a particular character, or are trying to convey a character's detachment, hiding their eyes can be a successful approach. However, if this is a moment in the film where you want the audience to feel a connection to the character, the audience must be able to clearly see their eyes.

In some cases, I will compose my antagonist's shots further off their eye line, closer to their profile, and my protagonist's shots closer to their eye line to maximize the connection to the protagonist and minimize the connection to the antagonist. This technique is so powerful that, in some cases, we will even be willing to forgive a character's actions just because we can see their eyes. My two favorite examples of this are *The Terminator* and *The Return of the Jedi*. In *The Terminator* we are introduced to a killing machine with absolutely no empathy or compassion. The character wears sunglasses throughout the film, limiting our emotional connection to him. *Terminator 2* begins in similar fashion, with the same leather-clad, sunglasses-wearing tough guy. Miraculously, in *Terminator 2*, when the Terminator becomes a good guy his sunglasses go missing, so we can clearly see his eyes. This allows us to form an emotional bond with the character. Trust me, this is not a coincidence; it is a carefully crafted choice by a calculating director.

The Return of the Jedi offers an even more dramatic example. For a combined five-and-a-half hours, through three films, the audience has watched Darth Vader kill almost everything that moves, going so far as to blow up an inhabited planet just to prove a point. This despicable character has no redeeming qualities, yet, at the end of *The Return of the Jedi,* Darth Vader decides to save his son, Luke, at the expense of his own life. At this point something incredible happens: Luke removes Darth Vader's helmet, and for the very first time, we see his eyes. He is no longer a killing machine, but rather a person, and just like that, we forgive him for all of the atrocities he has committed. This stands as a testament to two things: how great a film *The Return of the Jedi* is and how willing we are to forgive in film. The lesson is simple: Show your character's eyes!

CAMERA HEIGHT

Another important factor that is often overlooked by new filmmakers is the height of the camera. By simply changing the height of the camera, we can dramatically alter the way the audience feels about a character. It provides a subjective viewpoint and carries a great deal of impact. Remember, the camera, in many ways, is the audience's only perspective as a participant in the story, so use that to your advantage.

LOW-ANGLE SHOT

Placing the camera below a character's eyes makes them appear powerful and dominant. Because we as audience members must physically look up to them, it puts us in a subordinate position. In many ways, it is reminiscent of being a child and having to literally look up to our superiors. This can be done subtly to suggest dominance, or it can be done blatantly to make a character appear larger than life.

People often ask how low to place the camera, and my answer is always "Make it match the intensity and style of your film." If you have a highly stylized film with larger-than-life characters, you

FIG. 3.17. LOW-ANGLE SHOTS CONVEY A SENSE OF POWER.

can choose an extremely low angle. If your story is about "normal" people in believable situations, you should generally be more restrained. Remember, none of these directions will appear in the screenplay. It is solely up to the discretion of the director to make these decisions, and a good director will work tirelessly to create details like these to give the audience the visual information they need. What is amazing about this technique is that most audience members are emotionally aware of it, but not consciously aware of it. They feel it when it is being used, but they don't actually know why.

A few years ago I decided to conduct an experiment to test this theory. I showed my entry-level film students ten still images of characters in movies. All had either a high or low camera angle and I asked the students to write down if each character seemed powerful or weak. Without exception, all of the students answered the exact same way, all based on camera height. When pressed as to how they came to these conclusions, only three out of seventeen knew that camera height was the main factor. I heard other answers ranging from wardrobe to time period and even had one student answer that "The character looked powerful because of his mustache." We are fortunate that audience members have been conditioned to this technique; it makes our job as filmmakers just a little bit easier.

EYE-LEVEL SHOT

Placing the camera at eye level makes the audience feel as if they are equal to the characters. On a certain level, it makes the audience feel that the character is "us." That doesn't mean the protagonist must always be filmed at eye level; it just means that it's a good place to start. If the protagonist is then placed in a position of power, you can lower the camera, or if the protagonist is placed in a vulnerable position, you can raise the camera above eye level.

FIG. 3.18. EYE-LEVEL SHOTS CREATE A SENSE OF ONENESS WITH THE SUBJECT.

HIGH-ANGLE SHOT

Placing the camera above eye level makes the character seem vulnerable or weak. Unlike low-angle shots, you can only go so far above a character's eye level and maintain an emotional connection. Because of the shape of our faces, our brow ridge will block our eyes and we will lose that emotional connection. Not to worry! With this technique, a little bit goes a long way. The audience is extremely aware of this technique. As with all of the other rules, there are exceptions to this, one of which is the God's-eye view.

GOD'S-EYE VIEW

A God's-eye view shot is an extremely high-angle shot, looking straight down from above, as if it were God's perspective. This is often referred to as a "bird's-eye view shot" as well. This shot can be powerful when used to reveal the scale or size of a location or for showing the aftermath of a scene. For example, this could be used in a large battle scene to show the magnitude of the battle, or it could be used at the end of a battle scene to show the aftermath. Often filmmakers will start with a close-up God's-eye view and pull out to reveal more information. Although with a God's-eye view shot, we lose the direct emotional connection of seeing the eyes, we gain a larger perspective of the entire location and create a voyeuristic view as though we are seeing something without the character's knowledge.

FIG. 3.19. HIGH-ANGLE SHOTS CREATE A SENSE OF VULNERABILITY OR WEAKNESS.

FIG. 3.20. GOD'S-EYE VIEW SHOTS CREATE AN OTHER-WORLDLY AND VOYEURISTIC FEEL.

BALANCING A FRAME

Understanding how to properly fill your frame is another important rule that must be learned. In the beginning of your film-making career, this will be something you will need to put thought into each time you frame a shot, but just like the rest of the rules of composition, with time, this will become second nature. You will begin to feel whether or not your frame is balanced.

Balancing a frame is fairly simple. As we discussed, very rarely will our object or person of interest be placed in the center of the frame. This means that the frame will often feel weighted to the side that contains the object or person. This can make a frame seem uncomfortable and empty. The remedy? Place something on the opposite side of the frame to create a sense of balance and symmetry. Anything can be used: objects, furniture, people, shadows, etc. The key is making sure whatever you use doesn't distract from the main focus of the shot. A common technique is to place someone out of focus in the empty portion of the background. The audience won't be distracted and the frame won't seem empty.

An unbalanced frame is when you have your subject on one side of the frame and nothing on the other side of the frame. Creating an unbalanced frame is also a completely acceptable technique, but just like the other rules, it must be done correctly. Unbalanced frames make a character appear isolated and alone. Not just physically, but more importantly, emotionally. Although not all

FIG. 3.21. BALANCED FRAME.

FIG. 3.22. BALANCED FRAME.

FIG. 3.23. UNBALANCED FRAME.

FIG. 3.24. DUTCH ANGLE.

balanced frames contain multiple people, the simple act of placing an object in the frame with the character gives the appearance that they are not alone. A person alone in a frame can appear startlingly solitary. If you are trying to communicate to the audience that a character feels alone, this is an effective tool to use.

DUTCH ANGLE

The final technique we will cover in this chapter is the Dutch angle. A Dutch angle is when the camera is slightly tilted to one side or the other, causing the objects in the frame to look tilted. A Dutch angle is basically a way of telling the audience that something is wrong. It causes an uneasy feeling because it depicts the world the

audience has become accustomed to seeing, just slightly slanted. When used correctly, they are a powerful tool used masterfully by directors like Hitchcock, Welles and Spielberg. However, Dutch angles can feel extremely heavy-handed when used incorrectly, so use this tool sparingly.

More often than not, I find Dutch angles to be distracting and ineffective. The problem is that they are frequently executed incorrectly. One of the best pieces of advice I have ever been given was by an older cinematographer with whom I was working early in my career. His advice was twofold. The first part was to make sure the background of the frame has horizontal or vertical lines. A brick wall, stairs, vertical or horizontal blinds or curtains with a pattern all work well. The second and most important part was to have the actor lean in the same direction as the camera to counter the angle. For example, if you are tilting the camera to the left, have the actors lean the same direction. It will look and feel awkward on set, but what you are left with is a frame where the person appears to be standing perfectly vertical, while the lines in the background appear to slant. This way the person doesn't look off kilter, just the world around them does.

Remember, a Dutch angle should signify that there is something wrong with the world. Dutch angles, when used correctly, are a powerful tool; my warnings are not to dissuade you from using them, but rather to persuade you to use them wisely.

Composition is one of the most important tools we have as filmmakers. It will inform the audience of just as much detail as dialogue, but just like dialogue, you must be careful how you use it. Remember, everything in your frame matters. A slight change in camera height or framing can dramatically alter the way your audience feels, so be sure to put thought into each frame before you shoot. Don't be afraid to combine these techniques to maximize the information; they will all work together when combined properly. Lastly, have fun! Composition is your voice as a filmmaker, so don't be afraid to take risks . . . just know why you are taking them.

CHAPTER 4

THE CAMERA AS A STORYTELLING TOOL

Perhaps the most common misconception I hear from new directors (and some old-timers) is that camera and lenses are the cinematographer's territory. There seems to be a popular belief, even among many seasoned directors, that the director is responsible for working with the actors and choosing a frame, and the cinematographer makes the decisions regarding lighting, camera and lenses. Nothing could be further from the truth. Although it is the cinematographer's responsibility to master these tools, the director should be almost as knowledgeable.

There are few more powerful storytelling tools than cameras and lenses. These tools can transform the look and feel of any scene without a word of dialogue. Without a strong understanding of these techniques, a director is missing out on a crucial and necessary opportunity to communicate with his audience.

I have worked with many directors who rely heavily on their cinematographer to choose the type of lens that is to be used and although this is not uncommon, it is, in my opinion, a mistake. It is often said that each lens has its own "personality." A lens can make someone appear comical, or attractive, or even insane. It can stretch space, or compress it, as well as force the audience to look at a particular point of interest. The power of lens choice is rivaled by very few elements.

Understanding the basics of camera setting is just as important. So much of the look of a film is created within the camera these days, and a director *must* be a part of that discussion. For the better part of a century, the discussion revolved around what film stock to use and what frame rate to shoot, but with the invention of digital technology, the choices have become incredibly daunting. For this reason, directors don't need to concern themselves with knowing the ins and outs of all of the menu settings, but there are some basics that are universal from camera to camera. Color temperature, aspect ratio, ISO, resolution and shutter speed are a few that all directors should be comfortable with.

Let's start with some basics. Although many of you will already be familiar with some of this terminology, it is vital for everyone to understand when we begin discussing more advanced techniques.

EXPOSURE

Exposure is the amount of light that is captured by the image. There are many elements of a camera and lens that control exposure, and we will discuss them all, but first let's discuss what exposure actually is. Exposure is simply how bright or dark your image is. The three most basic levels of exposure are overexposure (the image is too bright), underexposure (the image is too dark), and proper exposure (the image is correctly exposed). There are, of course, degrees of each one of these levels, but these are the

blocks for which all degrees of exposure will be measured. There are reasons to use all three types of exposure, but more often than not, proper exposure is what we strive for.

However, when it comes to the overall frame, most frames will contain all three types of exposure. Generally, the point of interest will be properly exposed, while perhaps a window will be overexposed, and a dark corner of the room may be underexposed. That is what reality looks like. Take a look around you; there are always different levels of exposure in everyday life. Whether it is reflections from the sun, or shadows under a tree, there are always variables that will create variances in exposure. This is called "contrast." Contrast, which is the ratio between light and dark, is extremely pleasing to the eye and makes for a well-balanced frame. This is something we will cover in chapter 6.

OVER-EXPOSURE

When too much light is captured, it results in overexposure. Overexposure will make the image appear very bright, and in the case of complete overexposure, the image will turn white. When an overexposed image turns white, it signifies a complete loss of information, meaning that there is no image there. No matter what colors appear in an image, they will turn white when extremely overexposed. This is often referred to as a "blown out" image.

FIG. 4.1. OVER-EXPOSED IMAGE.

FIG. 4.2. UNDER-EXPOSED IMAGE.

UNDER-EXPOSURE

When not enough light is captured, the image will appear dark and when extremely underexposed, it will turn black. Just like overexposure, this means no image was captured. This lack of exposure will create a flat and boring look and will make it all but impossible to engage the audience.

PROPER EXPOSURE

Proper exposure is when the level of light matches the setting of the camera. Not everything must be properly exposed in a frame, but generally the more important elements should be. As I said

FIG. 4.3. PROPERLY EXPOSED IMAGE.

before, a properly exposed image will generally contain a combination of overexposure, underexposure and correct exposure, creating contrast and a dynamic image.

CONTROLLING EXPOSURE

There are many different ways of controlling exposure, so let's just begin with the basic in-camera adjustments.

IRIS

The first and most common way of adjusting exposure is to adjust the iris. The iris, also referred to as the "aperture," is a series of blades that form a ring inside the barrel of a lens. It is very similar to the pupil of an eye. This ring opens and closes to control how much light is allowed to enter the lens and strike the film or video sensor. All lenses have an adjustable aperture, which allows you to adjust the brightness of the image.

The wider the opening, the more light will be allowed to enter and strike the film or sensor of the camera. This will create a brighter exposure.

When the aperture is closed down, the image will get darker because less light is being allowed to enter.

These adjustments are made by turning a ring around the barrel of the lens (see figure 4.6).

These changes are not arbitrary; in fact, there is a measurement of each aperture variation. The measurements of aperture opening size, as well as amount of light entering the lens are called f-stops (sometimes referred to as T-stops). These f-stops are a scale of numbers and corresponding diameters.

F-stops are a complicated subject, so let's keep this simple. F-stops are a measurement of light. A high f-stop number means there is more light. A low f-stop number means there is less light. For

FIG. 4.4. OPEN APERTURE.

FIG. 4.5. CLOSED APERTURE.

FIG. 4.6. APERTURE RING.

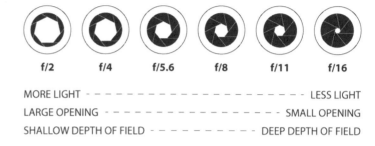

| f/2 | f/4 | f/5.6 | f/8 | f/11 | f/16 |

MORE LIGHT - LESS LIGHT
LARGE OPENING - - - - - - - - - - - - - - - - - SMALL OPENING
SHALLOW DEPTH OF FIELD - - - - - - - - DEEP DEPTH OF FIELD

FIG. 4.7. F-STOP SCALE SHOWS EFFECTS OF ADJUSTING THE APERTURE.

example, f/22 is much brighter than f/4. This concept can be confusing and counterintuitive because it is applied in two different ways: reading light and adjusting the aperture on the camera lens.

READING LIGHT

You will often see cinematographers holding a device that looks similar to a cell phone with a white bubble on top. This is a light meter. It is measuring the amount of light hitting a subject, which is why you will often see them hold the light meter in front of an actor's face. They are measuring the amount of light illuminating the actor. The light meter will show the cinematographer the amount of light measured in f-stops. If one side of the actor's face reads f/8 and the other side reads f/4, the side reading f/8 will be the brighter side. These measurements will directly correlate to the aperture of the camera.

ADJUSTING LIGHT

As I mentioned above, aperture settings are also measured in f-stops, so matching the aperture of the lens to the correct amount of light will give you proper exposure. For example, if your light meter reads f/4, you will set your lens aperture to f/4 for proper exposure. This is where things tend to get a bit confusing. If you increase the f-stop number on the lens from an f/4 to a higher number, (f/5.6, f/8, etc.) the image will get darker. This seems contradictory because when you are measuring light, the higher number indicates a brighter image. The exact opposite is true on a lens; increasing the f-stop number will darken the image, decreasing the f-stop number will brighten the image. This is because when you increase the f-stop number on the lens you are compensating for more light, which darkens the image (decreases the size of the opening).

Going back to our example of f/4, if you set the aperture to f/4 but decide you want your image to look a little darker, you would close the aperture to f/5.6 or higher. This means you are allowing less light to enter. If you decide you want to brighten your f/4, you would open the aperture to f/2.8 or lower. This means you are allowing more light to enter. The widest aperture of a lens, meaning how large you can make the iris opening or how low of an f-stop you can achieve, differs from lens to lens. Some lenses have a minimum aperture of f/1.4, while others may only open as wide as f/5.6.

You will often hear lenses referred to as either "fast" or "slow." A fast lens simply means that the widest aperture opens very wide like the f/1.4 lens. A slow lens means that the widest aperture isn't very wide. The f/5.6 lens would be an example of this. More often than not, the faster the lens, the more expensive it is. The subject of lenses and iris can be complicated, but the concept of aperture and f-stops will quickly become second nature to you with a little experience.

DEPTH OF FIELD

Although exposure is the main function of adjusting the aperture, there is an extremely significant secondary effect of adjusting the aperture. This secondary effect is depth of field. Depth of field is the distance between the nearest and farthest points of focus. A deep depth of field means that everything from the closest objects to the most distant objects in the frame will be in focus. A shallow

FIG. 4.8. F/1.4 (SHALLOW DEPTH OF FIELD).

FIG. 4.10. F/8 (SIGNIFICANTLY INCREASED DEPTH OF FIELD).

FIG. 4.9. F/4 (SLIGHTLY INCREASED DEPTH OF FIELD).

FIG. 4.11. F/16 (DEEP DEPTH OF FIELD).

depth of field means that focus could be as minimal as a single object in focus. Just like exposure, there aren't only deep or shallow depths of field, but rather degrees. You can have an extremely shallow depth or a slightly shallow depth of field. You can create a frame where a person's face is in focus and everything else is out of focus, or you can create a frame where just a person's eyes are in focus and everything else, including the rest of their face, is out of focus.

On the opposite end of the spectrum, you can create a frame where you have an entire group of people in focus, but the background is out of focus, or you can create a frame where you have the group and the background in focus. How do you control the depth of field? Well, it's actually quite simple. It breaks down like this: The higher the f-stop on the lens, the deeper the depth of field you will create. If the aperture is opened wider, to a lower f-stop number, the depth of field will become shallower.

Shooting at f/1.4 will create a very shallow depth of field, while shooting at f/2 will create a somewhat less shallow depth of field. Shooting at f/5.6 will create a somewhat deep depth of field, while shooting at f/11 will create an even deeper depth of field. So opening the aperture all the way to an f/1.4 will make the image brighter, and the secondary effect is that it will create a shallower depth of field. Closing down the aperture to f/11 will make the image darker, and the secondary effect is that it will create a deeper depth of field. This can be an extremely useful tool when it comes to drawing the audience's eye, but we will save that discussion for a later chapter.

Here's a quick summation I like to give my students to help them remember the effects of adjusting the aperture:

> The *lower* the f-stop number, the *wider* the aperture; and the *brighter* the image, the *shallower* the depth of field will be. The *higher* the f-stop number, the *narrower* the aperture; and the *darker* the image, the deeper the depth of field will be.

It's not great grammatically, but I've found it to be a valuable tool for memorization.

SHUTTER SPEED

Perhaps the second most common way of controlling light is by adjusting the shutter speed. The shutter is another concept that can be difficult to understand, but with a little experimentation, it too will make perfect sense. In order to understand what the shutter does, you must first understand that all cameras, both still or motion picture, work the exact same way. Despite the massive amount of menus or the fact that some shoot film while others use a digital sensor, they are all simply a box with a hole that opens and closes to capture an image. That's it. Sometimes when I'm working with a new, complicated camera system, I remind myself of that, and it removes some of the intimidation. The shutter, very simply, is the door that opens and closes to capture the image. Just like the aperture, the shutter will determine how bright or dark your image is; however, it works in a very different way. All cameras will have a method for adjusting the shutter, but rather than change the size of the opening, as with the aperture, you change the length of time the shutter is open. By adjusting the shutter speed, you are determining for how long the picture will be taken. The longer the shutter is left open, the brighter the image will be. The shorter length of time the shutter is left open, the darker the image will be. These times are measured in fractions of seconds. For example, the shutter speed 1/30 means the shutter will stay open for 1/30th of a second. A shutter speed of 1/1000 will be much darker than 1/30 because the shutter is open for a much shorter period of time.

Just like the aperture, the shutter also has a secondary effect. However, the secondary effect of adjusting the shutter is much more jarring than depth of field. When the shutter speed is adjusted, it will change the amount of motion blur in the image. For this reason, shutter speed is rarely adjusted to compensate for light. There are two types of motion blur. It can either be a streaking of moving objects, which comes from a very slow shutter speed, similar to when you take a photograph at night and anything moving is blurry. Alternately, it can be a staccato, jittery look that accompanies very fast shutter speeds.

FIG. 4.12.
SHUTTER
SPEED 1/48TH.

FIG. 4.13.
SHUTTER
SPEED 1/500TH.

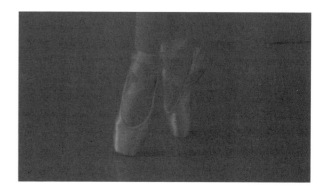

FIG. 4.14.
SHUTTER
SPEED 1/2000TH.

So how do you know if your shutter speed is too fast or too slow? In photography you can shoot at any shutter speed you choose, but in film, there are standard shutter speeds. If you are shooting at 24 frames-per-second (fps), the standard shutter speed is 1/48 (or 1/48th of a second). If you are shooting 30 fps, the standard shutter speed is 1/60 (or 1/60th of a second). If your shutter speed is slower than the standard shutter speed—for example if you are shooting 24 fps and your shutter speed is 1/15th of a second—you will likely have streaking across anything that is moving. If nothing is moving in the frame and the camera is completely still, the image will not blur. However, if anything in the frame moves, that object will streak or blur.

This is not necessarily a bad thing! Many films have used this effect to mimic hallucinations or similar effects. In addition to the motion blur, the image will become brighter because you are allowing the image to be exposed for a longer period of time.

If your shutter speed is faster than the standard shutter speed—for example, if your frame rate is 24 fps and your shutter speed is 1/500th of a second—and there is any movement in the frame, the movement will appear overly sharp and jittery, amplifying any movement. It will add a level of intensity to the images that the standard shutter speed cannot. Once again, this is not something to shy away from. Many action films use very high shutter speeds to give the scene a more dramatic effect. Oftentimes, this technique is used in chase scenes or fight sequences. The higher the shutter speed the more obvious this look will become. A shutter speed of 1/1000 will have a much more staccato effect than 1/100. In addition to the edgy look of the image, the exposure will also be darker as a result of the increased shutter speed.

Remember, adjusting your shutter speed can create a dramatic effect, but generally won't be your first line of defense for adjusting exposure. The side effect, motion blur, is just too noticeable. Adjusting the aperture is still a much better way of compensating for light. However, for creating dramatic looks, the shutter can be one of your biggest allies.

ISO AND GAIN

For those of you that come from a film or photography background, the concept of ISO should be a familiar one. The name stands for "International Organization for Standardization," which is simply the name of the organization that governs it, but it is one of the most valuable tools for controlling exposure.

Simply put, ISO controls the sensitivity to light of the camera sensor or film you are using. The ISO is often referred to as the "speed" of the film or camera sensor. Speed refers to the terminology "fast" and "slow" as we discussed earlier. The faster the film (or camera sensor) the more sensitive it is to light. The slower the film (or camera sensor), the more light it requires for proper exposure, just like lenses.

THE STANDARD ISO SCALE:

|50|100|200|400|800|1600|3200|6400|

Each time the ISO number doubles, the exposure will increase by one full f-stop.

This means ISO 400 will require one *more* f-stop of light than ISO 800, and ISO 1600 will require one *less* f-stop of light. This is extremely useful when shooting in low-light conditions.

I know this concept can seem difficult at first, so let's try to simplify a little more. If you have your aperture set to f/2 and your ISO speed set to 400, but your image looks too dark, increasing your ISO to

FIG. 4.16. ISO 400

FIG. 4.15. ISO 200

FIG. 4.17. ISO 800

Less sensitive (needs more light)					More sensitive (needs less light)		
50	100	200	400	800	1600	3200	6400
Fine Grain							Grainy/Noisey

FIG. 4.18. ISO AND CORRESPONDING VIDEO NOISE.

800 will make the image one f-stop brighter. If you then increase the ISO to 1600 it will be two f-stops brighter than the original image.

If this still doesn't make sense, grab a camera and start increasing the ISO. Many digital cameras will have an ISO adjustment, although some older cameras may not.

When shooting film, the process is a little different. Film has a predetermined ISO, so when purchasing film, you must consider what speed of film you are buying. If shooting in low-light conditions, you would want a fast film speed (high ISO number) and if shooting in bright daylight you would want a slower film speed (low ISO number). Many productions will shoot multiple film stocks to match the conditions of the various scenes.

Now that we have discussed the advantages of shooting at a high ISO speed, let's talk about the downside. As you increase your ISO (sensitivity), you will also increase the amount of video noise or grain. Video noise is degradation that looks like snow across the image.

FIG. 4.19. ISO 3200

FIG. 4.20. ISO 6400

It is extremely unpleasant to the eye, and as you increase the ISO the noise will exponentially increase. For this reason, it is always recommended that you shoot at the lowest possible ISO while still achieving proper exposure.

Some cameras won't have an adjustable ISO; instead, they will have a function called *gain*, which operates on the same principles as ISO, but is measured differently. It too increases the sensitivity to light of the camera but is measured in decibels instead of ISO speeds. Just like ISO, increasing the gain will add video noise to the image, degrading its quality. Just like ISO, you want to shoot with the lowest gain possible while still maintaining proper exposure.

Film grain—not to be confused with *gain*—is the side effect of choosing film with a high ISO and is very similar to video noise in that it lessens the image quality. However, it is often said that film grain is much more pleasing to the eye than video noise. Perhaps the reason is that film grain has a more neutral color. It appears almost as a layer of sand over the image. It is clearly visible but seems to blend in more with the image. It seems much more organic to the image, where video noise seems out of place. Grainy film is often chosen for stylistic reasons such as creating a dirty or gritty look. Video noise is rarely used as a stylistic choice.

Finding correct exposure is certainly not a simple task. It is a deliberate balancing act of adjusting aperture, shutter and ISO, but it is

fundamental to creating a compelling image. Incorrect exposure is one of the quickest ways of having your audience detach from your film. For this reason, correct exposure should always be a top priority. At first, you may find it confusing and intimidating. I know that I often found myself asking, "Should I adjust the aperture, or would adjusting the ISO be better?" Then I would have to consider the side effects of both approaches, which only seemed to complicate matters further. It can be a challenging process, but one that becomes effortless with time and experience. The complexities of exposure quickly become as second nature as breathing, and the decisions you make to achieve correct exposure become simple.

FRAME RATE

I have mentioned frame rate or frames per second a few times in this chapter without a proper explanation, so I will do so now. This concept can seem foreign to many new filmmakers because we so rarely shoot film these days, but the same concept applies to digital filmmaking as well. When shooting film, you are taking individual photographs in such a rapid succession that they appear to be moving images when played back. The number of these still images taken per second is your frame rate. The most common cinematic frame rate is 24 frames per second (fps). This includes movies, episodic television and music videos. Some television programming such as news, sitcom and reality shoot at 30 fps, although many have switched to 24 fps as well. You can shoot at other frame rates, as well, but be aware there is a dramatic side effect involving slow and fast motion.

SLOW MOTION AND FAST MOTION

Slow motion is a popular technique used in cinema, although there is some confusion as to how to achieve it. Many people believe that it is a post-production technique, but it works best when done in camera. To record slow motion, you simply shoot at a higher frame rate. For example, shooting at 48 fps rather than 24 fps will produce a slower image because the image will still be played back at 24 fps. When you record 48 fps and play it back at 24 fps, it gives the effect of slow motion because it takes twice as long to play back, since you have recorded twice as many frames. If you record at 72 fps, it will be three times slower since you have recorded three times as many frames. In addition to getting slower, the image will also get darker because you are exposing each frame for a shorter period of time.

Fast motion is the exact opposite. Shooting fewer frames per second will result in faster motion because it takes less time to play back. This effect is not utilized as often but is sometimes used for a comedic effect. Silent films were often shot at 12–18 frames per second, which is why they look so jumpy.

As cameras have become more advanced, their capabilities have increased exponentially. It was once considered astonishing to have a camera that could shoot 120 frames per second, but now there are cameras that shoot at over 25,000 frames per second at good resolution, and 1,000,000 frames per second at low resolution. Of course, that is a very specialized camera, but many prosumer-grade cameras these days will allow for some minor frame-rate changes.

RESOLUTION

Resolution is the information that makes up an image. It is made up of what are called "lines of resolution." These lines run both vertically and horizontally across the screen or camera sensor. Each one of these rows is simply a long line of pixels.

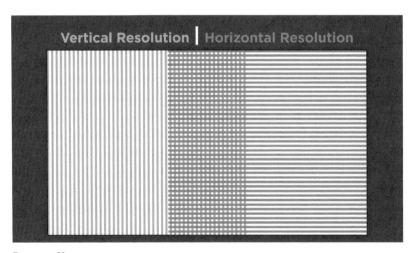

FIG. 4.21. HORIZONTAL AND VERTICAL ROWS OF PIXELS DETERMINE THE RESOLUTION OF THE IMAGE.

Anyone familiar with digital photography should be familiar with the concept of a pixel, which is the smallest unit of an image. Think about when you were a kid and you would sit too close to the television. Remember when you could see the little squares that made up the picture? Those squares were pixels. The amount of rows of pixels (lines of resolution) determine the resolution of your image. These resolutions are then referenced by their resolution count. For example, 1920 × 1080 is a resolution. 1920 represents the number of vertical lines of resolution making up the image, and 1080 represents the number of horizontal lines making up the image. These names are often shortened to just the horizontal number, in this case 1080p. (The "p" stands for progressive.)

Standard definition (the old square televisions most of us grew up with) has a resolution of 640 × 480 but is primarily noted as 480i (the "i" stands for interlaced). Early high definition recorded a resolution of 1280 × 720, commonly referred to as 720p. After 720p came 1440 × 1080 often referred to as 1080i, which was quickly followed by 1080p.

These days 1080i and 1080p are the most common high-definition formats, but this is quickly being replaced by much higher resolution cameras, monitors and televisions. Cameras with resolutions of 4K (4096 × 2160 or 3840 × 2160) and 8K (8192 × 4320 or 7680 × 4320) are manufactured by many different camera companies.

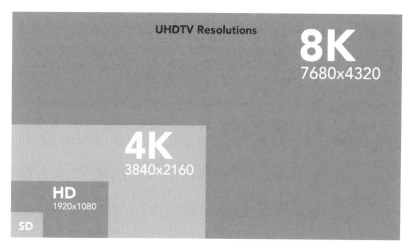

FIG. 4.22. RESOLUTION CHART.

So what is the appeal of higher resolution cameras? Well, an image with high resolution will have more pixels, and, therefore, smaller pixels. These smaller pixels result in a smoother looking image with less pixilation, resulting in a "cleaner" image. However, much of this is dependent upon the size of the screen on which the images will be shown. I like to equate resolution to a piece of rubber. If you have a small piece of rubber, you can only stretch it so far before it starts to break apart. If you have a larger piece of rubber, you can stretch it much farther. The larger the piece of rubber, the larger you can stretch it. The same thing is true with resolution: The more resolution you have, the larger you can stretch the image before it starts to break apart (pixilation). This means you can project higher resolutions on much larger screens without image degradation.

This is an important attribute if the final product is intended to be seen on a large screen. However, the difference between footage shot in 4k vs. footage shot in 1080p is indistinguishable on smaller screens. Much of our media these days is consumed on smartphones and tablets, and the pixels on these devices are far too small to make any discernible difference.

Resolution is much more noticeable when projected on a large movie screen. An audience will certainly see a difference between 720p and 1080p, as well as a noticeable difference between 1080p and 4k—so long as the image is projected in its true resolutions. The biggest problem there is that very few theaters actually have 4k or higher projectors. In most cases, footage that has been shot in 4k or higher must be down-converted to a lower resolution (generally 2k) to be screened.

I am often asked, "What resolution should I choose?" Unfortunately, there is no definitive answer to that question. You must consider the circumstances of your production to make an informed decision. The first variable you should consider is the intended final exhibition of your film. If you plan to screen your film in a theater with a 4k projector, then shooting and editing in 4k is your best option. If you are shooting a web series, then you most likely don't need to shoot in 4k, and 1080p will be more than enough resolution. As technology continues to advance, high resolution cameras will become increasingly more cost-effective; just be aware that shooting at extremely high resolutions will complicate the post-production process. Editing 4k and higher resolutions requires a very powerful computer as well as a massive amount of storage space.

The second consideration (although for many filmmakers, the first consideration) is budget. No matter what level of film you are making, you will almost always be constrained by the budget. Newer cameras with higher resolutions will almost always be more expensive to purchase or rent. Many filmmakers, myself included, have fallen into the trap of thinking we need the newest, highest resolution camera available. Perhaps you do, but ask yourself if choosing that camera will benefit the quality of your story. If the answer is no, then choose a camera that will.

ASPECT RATIO

There are many elements that make up a frame; one of the most important is the aspect ratio. The aspect ratio is the ratio of width to height of an image. More simply, it is the shape of the image. As you have probably noticed in your years of movie watching, sometimes the image is square, sometimes the image is widescreen and sometimes the image is extremely wide. This is a decision made by the director and should always be made in support of the story. You may be asking yourself, "How can the shape of the image affect the story?" Well, if you are shooting a film with sweeping landscapes, or large battle scenes, a very wide aspect ratio will allow you to show more of your geography. If you are shooting a film in confined locations with intimate moments, a narrower aspect ratio could benefit your story because it will allow you to get closer to your subjects with far less empty space in the frame. There are many standard aspect ratios and each one has a purpose.

First let's discuss how you measure aspect ratio. There are often two different formulas used, but both represent identical outcomes. The first aspect ratio is what many of us grew up watching: our old "square" televisions, which actually aren't truly a square image. This aspect ratio is most commonly referred to as 4:3. This means that it is four units wide by three units high. I am often asked, "How big is a unit?" There is no standard size. A unit could be the size of an ant or the size of a car depending on the size of the screen. All it means is that you have divided the width of the image into four identical units, and the height of the image into three identical units. This means that the image is one unit wider than it is high, making it slightly wide screen. You may also hear this shape referred to as 1.33:1. This is the exact same aspect ratio; it is simply being referenced in a different way. The last number, 1, represents the height of the image and 1.33 represents the width of the image. Very simply, the image is .33 times wider than it is tall.

An aspect ratio of 1.33:1 is rarely used these days because it was the native aspect ratio of standard definition. Standard definition was replaced by high definition and high definition has its own native aspect ratio. This aspect ratio is commonly referred to as 16:9. This means that it is sixteen units wide by nine units high. It is also sometimes called 1.77:1. Just like 1.33:1, this simply means that the image is .77 times wider than it is high.

The names 4:3 and 16:9 are most often used for these two formats when referencing television formatting, while 1.33:1 and 1.77:1 are the names most commonly used when referencing them as cinema aspect ratios. Either name is fine, as long as you understand what they mean. While 4:3 and 16:9 are the two most common television aspect ratios, there are two other aspect ratios that are used most often in cinema. The first and most popular is 1.85:1. This aspect ratio is slightly wider than 16:9 and is a favorite of many filmmakers. It allows for wide compositions, while it is still intimate enough for close-ups. The second most common cinema aspect ratio, 2.40:1, may also be referred to as 2.35:1, 2.37:1, or 2.39.1. They are all roughly the same aspect ratio, just slightly wider or narrower. This is a wonderful aspect ratio that creates an incredibly cinematic effect and allows for beautiful wide shots. It can, however, be challenging for close-ups because there is so much empty space left on the sides of the frame. I often see new filmmakers choose this aspect ratio solely because they believe it makes their movie look more professional. That is only the case if this aspect ratio fits your story.

The aspect ratio of a film is decided in pre-production and will rarely change through the duration of the film, although there are some exceptions to that rule. Some filmmakers will use changes in aspect ratios to represent changes within the story. A common

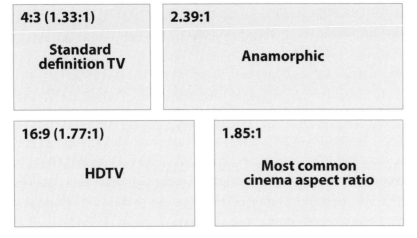

FIG. 4.23. THE MOST COMMONLY USED ASPECT RATIOS IN FILM AND TELEVISION.

technique is to use aspect ratio changes to represent different time periods. This is a very stylized technique, so be careful if you decide to employ it. Some cameras allow you to change the aspect ratio in camera. Others will have frame lines in the viewfinder that help you frame for a different aspect ratio. You then add black markers to create the aspect ratio for which you have framed. Whatever aspect ratio you choose, make sure it is always in support of your story.

COLOR TEMPERATURE

Another important consideration when creating images is color. Color can transform the time period of your film or make the audience feel the temperature of your location. It can make them feel at peace or terrified, all by choosing the right color. So what is the right color? Well, that, as I'm sure you've guessed, is not a simple question, but before we start using color to create emotion, we have to understand how to create images that appear "normal." We will discuss color over two chapters, this chapter and chapter 6.

Let's begin with some very simple information that everyone must know before lighting anything. We perceive most light to be "white light," meaning the light appears to be emitting a white or white-ish glow. Nothing could be further from the truth. In fact, most of these "white" lights have very distinct colors. So why do we see them as white? Well, our eyes have the amazing ability to convert all colored lights within a certain spectrum to what we see as white. This gives us a sense of continuity, so objects look the same under most lighting conditions.

Color of light is measured in temperatures known as degrees "Kelvin," which is represented by the letter K next to each number. The Kelvin scale was developed in the late 1800s by William Kelvin. His goal was to quantify colors of light and to do so he heated a block of carbon. It glowed in the heat, producing a range of different colors at different temperatures. When heated, the carbon began to glow red. As the temperature increased, the carbon began to glow a bright yellow and eventually turned to a bright blue-white glow. The lower the temperature number, the warmer the light. The higher the temperature number, the bluer the light.

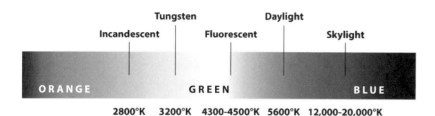

FIG. 4.24. COLOR TEMPERATURE SCALE.

On this scale you will see the most common color temperatures used in filmmaking. Tungsten, the type of light used most often by filmmakers, burns at 3200 degrees Kelvin. This generates an orange-ish light. As the Kelvin temperature increases, the light will drift toward the blue end of the spectrum. Think of it like a flame. An orange flame, although hot, is not as hot as a blue flame. Daylight is 5600 degrees Kelvin and a blue light. This is the other most common color temperature in film. Computer monitors emit an even bluer light, and are measured around 6500 degrees Kelvin, while shade is roughly 10,000 degrees Kelvin. This can be confusing because daylight is 5600K. The difference is that daylight is direct sunlight shining on an object, while shade is the light that is indirect sunlight, such as light under a tree. This light is much more blue than direct sunlight.

The most common question I get when discussing color temperature is, "Why does this matter?" This matters because a camera does not function like the human eye. When we see daylight, it looks white, as do tungsten and fluorescent lights. Our eyes and brains can balance these colors automatically. However, a camera cannot.

This surprises many new filmmakers when they flip on their camera and can't figure out why all of the colors look out of whack. Generally, the image will either look very orange or very blue. Sometimes they will get lucky and the camera will be set to the correct color temperature, but this is not something to leave to chance. You should always set your color temperature appropriately. This process is called "white balancing" the camera.

Most cameras will have a few white balance functions. The first is "auto white balance." It will do its best to read the lighting conditions and adjust accordingly. On many cameras, it's quite accurate; however, I try to avoid this whenever possible. Here's an example of why. Let's say you are shooting in a room filled with tungsten light. The auto white balance will set itself to tungsten. If you then pan the camera past a window, the camera will switch itself to daylight. This will make all of the colors in the image shift. Auto white balance may be useful in certain situations, but I try and stay away from using any auto functions of a camera. Part of the fun of being a filmmaker is getting to be a control freak. So why would you want a camera to tell you how the image should look?

The next white balance function you will likely encounter is preset white balances. These can be very useful. They are preset color temperatures for various conditions such as daylight and tungsten.

I find the tungsten to be most useful because tungsten lights burn at a fairly consistent color temperature, while the temperature of daylight changes throughout the day.

Another white balance setting is manual white balance, which I find to be the most useful. This means you are telling the camera the exact white balance color temperature to set the camera. Depending on the camera, there are generally two different ways this can be achieved. The first is by holding a white sheet of paper or card in front of the camera. NOTE: make sure the white paper is being lit by the lighting conditions in which you will be shooting. (Example: If you are shooting under tungsten light, make sure the paper is being lit by that tungsten light.)

FIG. 4. 25. WHITE BALANCING A CAMERA.

Next, press the button designated for custom or manual white balance. What you will see is the paper turn white on the screen or in the viewfinder. What you are doing is telling the camera, "This paper is white, so adjust everything accordingly," which is exactly what the camera does. The other way of setting a custom white balance is by actually dialing in the exact Kelvin number you want to use. Not all cameras have this function, but it can be very useful for fine-tuning colors. When a camera is white balanced correctly, the colors in the image will appear lifelike and natural.

So let's talk about what happens when white balancing is done incorrectly. First, you must understand the nature of color. All light is made up of three primary colors: red, green, and blue (R.G.B.). When combined, these three colors make white light. It's strange the first time you see it, but pointing those three colors of light on one spot will actually create a white light. When two of the primary colors are combined, they make secondary colors. Each color will also have a complementary color. Each color when combined with its complementary color will create white light. The easiest way to find a color's complementary color is to look on a color wheel. The color directly opposite your color is its complementary color.

White balance works on the primary/complementary system. For example, if you set the camera to tungsten white balance, the camera is expecting orange light to enter the lens because tungsten light is orange. In order to compensate for the orange light

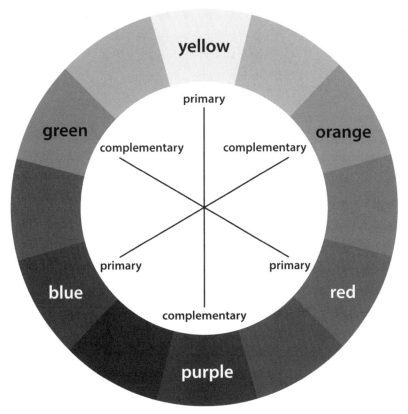

FIG. 4.26. COLOR WHEEL.

for the incoming orange light by turning the image blue. (Blue is the opposite of orange on the color spectrum.) The combination of orange light and blue light creates white light, creating a neutral looking image. The exact opposite happens when the camera is switched to the daylight setting. Since daylight is blue, the camera turns the image orange to compensate for the blue daylight.

When the wrong color temperature is selected, the colors appear incorrect. For example, if you are shooting in daylight conditions but have the camera set to tungsten, the image will appear overly blue. Setting the camera to tungsten tells the camera to expect orange light, so in return, the camera turns the image blue to balance out for the orange light. The problem is that daylight is also blue. That is why you are left with a very blue image. When using tungsten lights and the daylight setting, the opposite will happen. The image will turn orange. The best approach is to check your white balance before, during, and after shooting to ensure your camera is set correctly.

entering the lens, the camera turns the image the exact opposite or complementary color. In the case of tungsten, the opposite or complementary color is blue.

Once more, for clarity: Tungsten light is orange. When the camera is set to the tungsten setting, the camera compensates

USING COLOR TO ENHANCE THE STORY

Now let's get to the fun part of adjusting color temperature. There will undoubtedly be times in your career when you are trying to create a particular look for your film: perhaps an overall hue to your image, like orange, blue, or green. This is where white balance manipulation can help. Let's say you want to create a green look for your film. Now that you understand the principles of the color wheel, you can achieve this look. All you have to do is find the opposite or complementary color and white balance to that. In this case, the opposite of green is magenta. There are two different ways of white balancing to magenta or any other color.

The first is to find a magenta piece of paper to use as your white card.

The second is to find a magenta gel and hold that in front of the lens; then use a white sheet of paper for the white balance process. Either approach will give you green. White balance manipulation is fantastic for creating distinct looks, but be aware that this will tint the entire image whatever color you choose. This is not the same as putting a colored gel over a light, which will only change the color of that light. It is often best to shoot with a clean image and manipulate colors in editing. Changing colors in-camera can make color correction much more difficult.

Camera manufacturers have made great technological advancements over the past two decades. Technology has created so many opportunities for storytellers to achieve things that were once only possible in our minds. It has allowed filmmakers to create new universes that two decades ago would have been unimaginable. It has also made filmmaking accessible to people who once thought of it as nothing but a pipe dream. Although technology can greatly enhance the quality of a film, it should never be seen as a replacement for a great story. The goal is to use technology to enrich our films.

CHAPTER 5

LENSES AND FOCUS

Lenses are one of the most powerful storytelling tools we as filmmakers have at our disposal. There are thousands of types of lenses available and each one will have its own characteristics and personality. I often find that directors underestimate the power of lens choice and focus their attention elsewhere. I cannot stress enough how important it is for directors and cinematographers to be extremely comfortable with lens characteristics. Lenses break down into a few different categories, all of which have specific purposes.

WIDE ANGLE VS. TELEPHOTO

The first category when discussing lenses is wide angle vs. telephoto lenses.

Wide-Angle Lenses: A wide-angle lens creates what is called a wide field of view. Field of view is what is visible in the frame from side to side and top to bottom.

A wide-angle lens will allow you to see a large area or field of view. This can be exceptionally useful when shooting in confined spaces like the interior of a car or a small room.

Wide-angle lenses also stretch space, which means anything close to a wide-angle lens will look very close and very large. Anything farther away will look very small and very far away. This phenomenon is called "forced perspective." Forced perspective is an optical illusion created by wide-angle lenses. It

FIG. 5.1. WIDE-ANGLE LENS CREATES A WIDE FIELD OF VIEW.

FIG. 5.2. WIDE-ANGLE LENS STRETCHES SPACE.

distorts perspective, changing the size and angle of objects. In Fig. 5.1, notice how the aisle between the seats narrows as it gets farther away from the camera. This is a result of forced perspective. The farther away from the lens an object is, the smaller it will appear. The end of the row of seats is farther from the lens so it looks more narrow.

In Fig. 5.2 the girl in the foreground appears substantially larger that the man in the middle ground because of the forced perspective of the wide-angle lens. This creates the notion that the girl is far more important than the man, even though we are only seeing her back. Forced perspective can be a useful technique when trying to create a unique perspective, because this is simply not how the human eye renders images. It gives the audience a distinctive view of the world and allows a filmmaker to emphasize particular portions of the frame.

Telephoto Lenses: Telephoto lenses, also known as "long" lenses, have the exact opposite effects. They have a very narrow field of view, almost like looking through a paper towel roll. They do not allow you to see very far from side to side, only straight ahead. Telephoto lenses also magnify the image more than wide-angle lenses.

Unlike wide-angle lenses, which stretch space, telephoto lenses compress space. Objects close to the camera

FIG. 5.3. TELEPHOTO LENS CREATES A NARROW FIELD OF VIEW.

FIG. 5.4. WIDE-ANGLE LENS (LESS COMPRESSION).

and objects farther away look closer together than they actually are. For example, in a shot with a person in the foreground and a person thirty feet behind them, the two subjects will look much closer together than they actually are because of this compression.

Wide-Angle Lenses	Telephoto Lenses
Wide Field of View	Narrow Field of View
Stretches Space	Compresses Space
Distorted (Forced) Perspective	Flattering Perspective

FIG. 5.5. TELEPHOTO LENS (MORE COMPRESSION).

ZOOM LENSES VS. PRIME LENSES

Zoom lenses: Most people are familiar with zoom lenses. This type of lens is able to change focal lengths or magnify/widen the image. Simply put, if an object seems too far away or too small in the frame, you can zoom in to make the image appear closer and larger. A zoom lens can change from a wide-angle lens, to a medium-angle lens, and all the way to a telephoto lens, just by pressing a button or turning the zoom ring. This happens by changing the distances between glass elements within the lens. Zoom lenses can be very useful because they give you the option of many focal lengths built into one lens.

Prime Lenses: This lens type is less commonly seen outside of the professional photography and filmmaking world because they require more work and expertise than zoom lenses. A prime lens, also known as a fixed focal-length lens, does not zoom in or out. Whatever distance or size an object appears in your frame is the size it will be unless the camera or object is moved. For example, if you want a close-up of a person's face but they are currently in a wide shot, you would have to decrease the distance between the person and the camera or change to a more magnified prime lens. With a zoom lens, all you would have to do is zoom into a close-up. Prime lenses come in different focal lengths, which are basically levels of magnification.

These levels of magnification are measured in millimeters (mm). The lower the mm number, the more wide-angle the lens. The higher the mm number, the more magnified the image will be. A zoom lens would offer all of these choices within the same lens. This can be very convenient when fine-tuning your shot, because you don't have to pick up the camera and move it, change the positioning of the actors or switch lenses.

So why would anyone use a prime lens? Well, there are some unique advantages for using a prime lens over a zoom lens. The first advantage is prime lenses are generally faster than zoom lenses. If you remember the terminology fast vs. slow, this means that most prime lenses are more sensitive to light than zooms because they often have a wider maximum-aperture opening. They are also generally much smaller and lighter than zoom lenses as well. A professional filmmaking zoom lens can be as large as three feet long and weigh as much as twenty pounds. The final major advantage of using a prime lens over a zoom lens is that they often create a sharper image than zoom lenses. This is because zoom lenses often have more glass elements that the light must pass through before hitting the sensor of the camera. Each element will slightly soften or dull the image. This is also the reason that zoom lenses are often slower than prime lenses. Each time the light passes through a layer of glass, it loses a small amount of light.

So which lens should you use? Most often on a film set there will be a wide array of lenses. Generally, you will have a kit of prime lenses ranging from wide angle to medium and telephoto, as well as a zoom lens. The standard lens kit I use is generally an 18 mm, 24 mm, 35 mm, 50 mm, 85 mm and a 135 mm. Some lens manufacturers have variations of these lens sizes. Some will make a 90 mm instead of an 85 mm and a 28 mm instead of a 24 mm, etc. I will also often have a large zoom lens as well. Generally, though, I will stick to prime lenses unless I am actually zooming during the shot or my most telephoto prime lens isn't telephoto enough. Recently, many lens manufacturers have created zoom lenses that are just as sharp as prime lenses and almost as fast. If you are working on a budget, or are in a run-and-gun situation, there are many wonderful zoom lenses on the market.

PICKING THE CORRECT LENS

Now that we understand the categories and types of lenses, let's talk about how using the correct lens can help to tell your story. As we have discussed, creating strong visuals with a message is the job of every filmmaker. Choosing the right lens will either communicate your message or confuse it. It is often said that a telephoto lens should be used for close-ups, while wide-angle lenses should be used for wider shots. Although this can be true, it is certainly not a requirement. Any lens can achieve any size shot. A telephoto lens filming a person may give you a close-up, but if

you move the camera back far enough it will now give you a full shot. In reverse, a wide-angle lens filming a person may give you a wide shot, but if moved close enough, you can achieve a close-up. So why does it matter which lens you choose? Well, remember the characteristics of each lens will be different. Telephoto lenses when filming a close-up of a person's face are often called "beauty lenses" because the compression is very flattering. It makes people's facial features appear proportionate.

A close-up using a wide-angle lens will do the exact opposite. Remember, wide-angle lenses stretch space, so anything close to a wide-angle lens will look big and anything farther away will look smaller. Because you would have to place a wide-angle lens very close to a person's face for a close-up, it exaggerates the features,

FIG. 5.6. TELEPHOTO CLOSE-UPS ARE VERY FLATTERING.

FIG. 5.7. WIDE-ANGLE CLOSE-UPS DISTORT HUMAN FEATURES.

making the nose look huge and the eyes look smaller. Again, this is not necessarily a mistake but rather a stylistic choice.

A telephoto close-up will make your character appear attractive, while a wide-angle close-up will make your character appear awkward and uncomfortable.

Both shots are close-ups, but as you can see, they are telling two completely different stories. The same thing can be said for wide shots. A telephoto wide shot will give a completely different effect than a wide-angle wide shot. A wide-angle wide shot will allow the audience to see the space around the person because of the wide field of view, which is great for establishing geography. A

telephoto long shot will focus more on the subject and show less of the geography because of the narrow field of view.

A wide-angle lens, in almost any situation, will make us feel like we are physically closer to whatever we are seeing because the camera is in fact closer. Many great filmmakers choose to use wide-angle close-ups and medium shots for this very reason. It makes the audience feel like they are physically closer to the characters, which in turn makes them feel emotionally closer to the characters. We don't always necessarily want to feel closer; sometimes shooting on a long lens gives us an emotional distance that suits the scene.

Lens choice isn't just important for close-ups. You must consider your lens choice for all shot sizes and types. For example, if a shot consists of two people talking and you are filming from over one of the character's shoulders, lens choice will play a significant role. A wide-angle lens will increase the distance between the two characters, while a telephoto lens will compress the two people together. These two choices will create dramatically different emotions for the audience.

Also, understand that there is not just one size of wide-angle or telephoto lenses. Lenses come in many different focal lengths.

The categories are as follows:

Super-Wide Angle (12–18 mm)
Wide Angle (21–28 mm)
Normal (35–50 mm)
Telephoto (75–135 mm)
Super Telephoto (200+ mm)

Not only are there lens variations between focal lengths, there are variations between image characteristics. Some lens manufacturers strive for an extremely sharp and crisp image, while others like a softer, creamier effect. Some will create a slightly cool color while others have a warmer tone. I have found that my lens choice is based heavily on the emotion I'm hoping to create. Until recently, great prime lenses were often out of reach for independent filmmakers on a tight budget, but in the past few years, many new lens manufacturers have begun selling far less expensive, high-quality lenses. This has given filmmakers much more flexibility in their storytelling.

Lenses will not make a bad film into a great film, but they can certainly enhance your storytelling capabilities. Lens choice is not arbitrary, nor is it solely the cinematographer's decision. Every director should be capable of making an informed and thoughtful decision. This ability comes from experience. When learning your lenses, your best bet is to simply experiment. Decide what shot size you want (close-up, medium, full shot) and try it on many different lenses. Try it on a telephoto lens, then put on a wide-angle lens, move closer and find the exact same shot size. If you are using a zoom lens, follow the exact same approach; just change your focal length instead of changing your lens. Over time, you will begin to feel the different emotional effects. I am an absolute lens junkie both in my photography and cinematography. I love the emotional weight and non-verbal power communicated by each lens. The possibilities and combinations are truly endless.

CHAPTER 6

LIGHTING

Covering the theory of lighting in one book is a challenge, but covering lighting in one chapter is completely impossible. For this reason, we'll only be examining lighting from a storyteller's perspective. Although lighting is the cinematographer's responsibility, this chapter should not be seen as a chapter on cinematography alone. All of the concepts we will discuss are just as relevant for the director as they are for the cinematographer.

When I was first starting out in the film industry, I tried my best to make everything look incredible. I loved using lots of bright vivid colors and high-contrast lighting. I thought the more noticeable my work was, the more attention I would draw. This was true; however, it was the wrong kind of attention. One day on set the director took me aside and said, "What are you doing?" I replied, "Lighting the scene." He then asked, "When is the last time you saw anyone lit by a purple glow?" I realized in that moment that my approach had been all wrong. Cinematography should be invisible to the general audience. As soon as they are aware of it, the magic vanishes.

I quickly realized that a bad cinematographer tries to create noticeable, over-the-top images. They focus on making their images look striking. There is nothing wrong with trying to create bold images, but that should never be your main goal.

A good cinematographer strives to create images that tell the story. Not all films call for bright, beautiful, saturated pictures. Some films benefit from low-contrast images or muted colors. Ask yourself what type of story you are telling and then work to create that world.

The difference between a good cinematographer and a great cinematographer is that a great cinematographer can create bold and powerful images that also fit the story. The lighting doesn't distract from the story, but rather, enhances it. It creates a visually striking world through intricate means of which the audience is unaware. When a cinematographer is able to achieve this, it is a powerful thing.

Let's simplify: A bad cinematographer tries to create striking images but pays little attention to story, often creating unmotivated images. A good cinematographer tries to tell the story using visuals, creating images that match the tone of the story. A great cinematographer achieves both goals at the same time, creating bold, striking and, most importantly, motivated images.

CONTRAST

There are many different types of light and styles of lighting, but one thing is almost always true: You should never place a light on the same axis as the camera. To simplify, never point a

FIG. 6.1. FLAT LIGHTING.

FIG. 6.2. HIGH-CONTRAST LIGHTING.

light and a camera at the same object from the same angle. The reason? Shadows. Shadows are one of the most important elements of lighting. In fact, 50% of lighting is shadows. Generally, the more shadow you have, the more dramatic the film will look. The problem with pointing a light and a camera at the same spot is that all of the shadows will be behind the object, where the camera can't see them. This creates flat, boring images that are extremely uncinematic. I once heard a veteran of lighting say, "Shining a light on someone isn't lighting, it's illuminating. Lighting is the art of taking light away." Creating shadows is what lighting is all about. It is a major element of creating drama and emotion in a story.

The concept of creating shadows is called contrast. Very simply put, contrast is the ratio between light and dark. For example, when lighting a person's face, if the entire face is equally lit, there is no contrast. If half of the face is bright and the other half is slightly darker, that is low contrast. If one side of the face is brightly lit and the other side is pitch black, that is high contrast. Creating contrast is an important part of lighting and oftentimes the story or scene will dictate how much contrast you need.

HIGH KEY VS. LOW KEY

On set, high contrast or low contrast are often referred to as high key or low key. A high-key image is the same as a low-contrast image. The image will be fairly evenly lit. High-key images are often brightly lit, but that is not a requirement. The only condition is that it has low contrast. A low-key image is the same as a high-contrast image. It will have dark shadows and lots of contrast.

Generally, comedies, romantic comedies and love stories will be lit high key, while dramas, thrillers, and horror films are often lit low key. Although this is the norm, any genre of film can be lit high or low key. There are some very famous horror films that have been lit high key with beautiful soft light with very effective results. You'll see this, for example, in *The Shining*, *The Texas Chainsaw Massacre*, and *The Hills Have Eyes*. In order to achieve contrast, you must understand where to place the lights.

THREE-POINT LIGHTING

Three-point lighting is a common technique for achieving a balanced and pleasing appearance. As I'm sure you've guessed, three-point lighting is made up of three lights. Although it is the first concept we will cover, it is not the only technique for lighting. Sometimes a scene will call for three-point lighting. Other times a scene may call for one-point lighting or many points of light. Every scene is different, but three-point lighting is a great place to start because it introduces the three main types of lights: Key light, fill light, and back light.

KEY LIGHT

The first light is called the key light and it will always be the brightest light hitting your subject. Every lighting setup will have a key light regardless if it's three-point lighting or one hundred–point lighting. Think of it this way; if you were standing under a street light on a sunny day, the sun would be your key light, even if the street light was illuminated. Why? Because the sun is brighter. If you switched that scene and made it a nighttime scene, even on a full moon, the street light would now become the key light because it is brighter than the moon. There are no rules dictating where a key light *must* be placed, but there are some things a filmmaker should know.

First: The farther away from the axis of the camera you place the key light, the more contrast you will create. Forty-five degrees off axis of the camera is a great place to start. This will give some contrast, avoiding flat lighting, but not too much contrast. From there, you can decide if more or less contrast is needed.

A 50/50 places the light directly at the profile of the subject and makes half of the subject lit and the other half in shadow, thus the name 50/50. This type of lighting is great for lighting dramatic scenes or scenes in which you want to create a disconnect from your character. The disconnect comes from the fact that you can see very little of the character's eyes.

FIG. 6.3. 45-DEGREE LIGHTING.

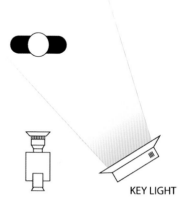

KEY LIGHT

FIG. 6.4. LIGHT IS PLACED 45 DEGREES OFF-AXIS.

FIG. 6.5. 50/50 LIGHTING.

FIG. 6.7. THREE-QUARTER BACKLIGHT.

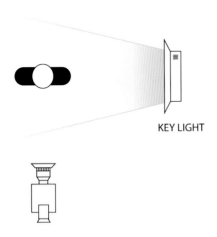

KEY LIGHT

FIG. 6.6. LIGHT IS PLACED 90 DEGREES OFF-AXIS.

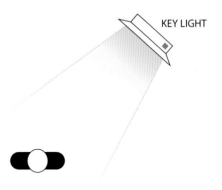

KEY LIGHT

FIG. 6.8. LIGHT IS PLACED ROUGHLY 130 DEGREES OFF-AXIS.

FIG. 6.9. BACKLIGHTING.

KEY LIGHT

FIG. 6.10. LIGHT IS PLACED BETWEEN 140 DEGREES AND 180 DEGREES OFF-AXIS.

Placing the camera about 130 degrees off-axis is called a three-quarter backlight because most of the light is hitting the back of the subject. The face receives very little light. For this reason, the three-quarter backlight is great for lighting mysterious or dangerous characters.

The farthest off axis you can go is to place the key light directly behind the subject. This technique is called backlighting, in which the light directly hits the back of the subject. It shines even less light on the face than the three-quarter backlight. It is an even better way of hiding a person's identity, emotional state, or making them mysterious.

Backlighting is often confused with silhouette lighting, but the two are, in fact, different. Silhouette lighting is when the background behind the person is brightly lit and the person or subject is dark. The difference is that the light is no longer shining on the back of the person but rather the background behind them. Silhouette lighting creates a softer effect, where backlighting creates a slightly more dramatic and intense look. If you have a dark background, a backlight is the best technique. If you have a light background, you can use either a silhouette or a backlight.

Both ways produce a similar effect, but backlighting can often give a more ethereal or angelic quality because of the halo effect caused by the light.

FIG. 6.11. SILHOUETTE LIGHTING.

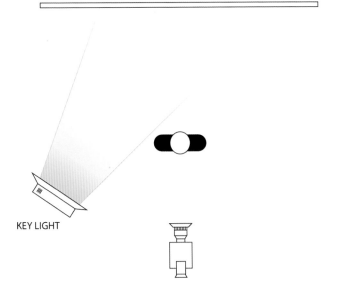

KEY LIGHT

FIG. 6.12. LIGHT DIRECTED AT BACKGROUND INSTEAD OF SUBJECT.

Next: Consider the height of the light. Key lights are generally placed above the eye-level of the subject. We almost always light from above when shooting. Generally, we place a key light above because it is most often where we are lit from in reality. When we are outside during the day, we are almost always going to be lit by the sun, and when we are inside, we are almost always going to be lit by overhead lighting. We are used to seeing life lit this way, so it feels comfortable to see films lit this way as well. A good starting point is 45 degrees above the actor's eye level. This angle of light creates an attractive "realistic" look.

While this is the most common positioning of a key light, it is not the only option. Lighting from below eye level or "up-lighting" is also a very popular technique. Up-lighting is most often used in horror or thriller films when you are trying to make a character look scary. This technique is reminiscent of being a kid and holding a flashlight under your chin while telling ghost stories. It creates a ghoulish effect because the light hits places on the face we are not accustomed to seeing lit. It is a fantastic tool for making the audience feel afraid of a character. The audience understands what up-lighting means on an emotional level, but very few audience members are ever consciously aware of it. Although it is effective, it should be used only when it helps to tell the story. If used for the wrong reasons it will surely confuse or misdirect your audience.

FIG. 6.13. KEY LIGHT PLACED 45 DEGREES OFF AXIS CREATES A NATURAL AND BALANCED LOOK.

FIG. 6.15. UP-LIGHTING CREATES A DRAMATIC EFFECT.

FIG. 6.14. KEY LIGHT PLACED 45 DEGREES ABOVE THE EYE-LEVEL OF SUBJECT.

FIG. 6.16. LIGHT PLACED BELOW EYE-LEVEL TO CREATE UP-LIGHT EFFECT.

TOP LIGHT

Top-lighting is another technique that is widely used in cinema. Top-lighting simply means you are placing your key light directly above the subject, pointing straight down at the top of their head. This is a great technique for hiding a person's eyes because you will still be able to see their face, but because of their brow ridge, no light reaches their eyes. If you want to know what parts of the face will get lit with this type of lighting, simply flatten out your hand and run it down your face from forehead to chin. Anything you touch will be lit; anything you don't will be dark. As we discussed in chapter 3, hiding a character's eyes can be useful when trying to hide their emotional state or when trying to make the audience feel disconnected from them. As we know, if we can't see a character's eyes, it will be difficult to connect with them on an emotional level.

It's incredible how dramatically the mood of the scene can be changed just by adjusting the height of the key light.

FILL LIGHT

The second light in the three-point lighting setup is called the fill light. The fill light is used to fill in the shadows created by the key light. The trick to a successful fill light is to make sure it isn't as bright as the key light. If the intensity of the two lights is the same,

FIG. 6.17. TOP-LIGHTING HIDES THE EYES, CREATING A MYSTERIOUS EFFECT.

FIG. 6.18. LIGHT PLACED DIRECTLY ABOVE TOP OF THE HEAD TO CREATE A TOP-LIGHTING EFFECT.

FIG. 6.19. KEY LIGHT WITH NO FILL LIGHT.

FIG. 6.21. FILL LIGHT INCORPORATED TO FILL IN SHADOWS CREATED BY THE KEY LIGHT.

FIG. 6.20. KEY LIGHT ONLY.

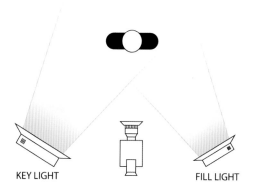

FIG. 6.22. KEY LIGHT AND FILL LIGHT.

FIG. 6.23. FILL LIGHT PLACED OPPOSITE THE KEY LIGHT.

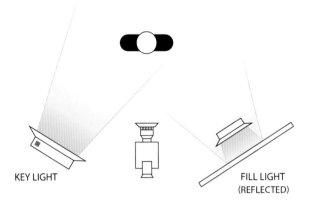

FIG. 6.24. REFLECTED (OR BOUNCED) FILL SOFTENS THE LIGHT.

you will create a flat, washed-out look. If the fill light is brighter than the key light, you have now just changed the fill light into your key light. There is no correct amount of fill light to use, but remember that the more fill light you use, the less contrast your image will have. A fill light will almost always come from the opposite side of the camera than the key light, but there are, of course, exceptions.

Some images require no fill light because a low-key look is the desired effect. Other times, the shadow created by the key light is just too strong. It is up to you as a filmmaker to decide how much fill light your subject requires. The simplest way of determining this is to ask yourself what type of character and story

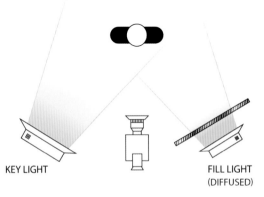

FIG. 6.25. DIFFUSION IS THE PROCESS OF SHINING A LIGHT THROUGH TRANSLUCENT MATERIAL TO SOFTEN THE LIGHT.

you are lighting. If it is a hard or dangerous character, you will most likely want less fill light. If it's a soft or kind character, you may want more fill light. There are many different techniques for creating a fill light, but the three most common are using a light that is not as bright as your key light, using a reflector to bounce light back onto the subject, or shining a light through diffusion to soften the light.

BACKLIGHT

The final light in three-point lighting is the backlight. The backlight, as we discussed before, is a light that shines on the back of a subject.

Using a backlight when key lighting a subject has a different effect than simply creating a mysterious subject. What a backlight does when used in conjunction with a key light is create a more three-dimensional look. Often, when a backlight is not used, a subject will blend in with the background. This makes the images look flat and un-lifelike. The reason this happens is that the exposure of the subject's hair and the exposure of the background is often similar.

When a backlight is added, it creates a difference in exposure, which in turn creates a separation between the subject and background. It shows the actual distance between the subject and the

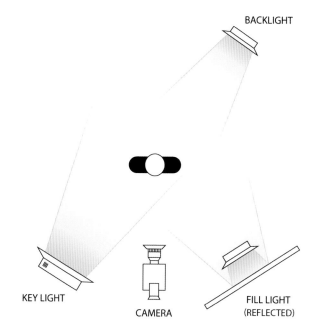

FIG. 6.26. ADDING A BACKLIGHT CREATES THREE-POINT LIGHTING.

background as well as creating depth in the frame. Some filmmakers love to use backlights for this very reason, while others prefer a more natural look. I have encountered many cinematographers that feel backlights don't look natural and, therefore, avoid them. I choose to use backlights on a situational basis. If I can justify using a backlight, I will. If not, I will forgo the use of a backlight and try to place a light shining on the background to create a similar effect.

FIG. 6.27. WITHOUT BACKLIGHT.

FIG. 6.29 KEY LIGHT, FILL LIGHT AND BACKLIGHT CREATE A BALANCED FEEL.

FIG. 6.28. WITH BACKLIGHT.

As we discussed before, three-point lighting is a useful technique but not required for every scene. It is often used for sit-down interviews because of its balanced look, but many scenes will benefit from other styles of lighting. Just remember, the terminology and techniques are universal no matter how many lights you may be using. A key light will always be referred to as a key light no matter how many lights you are using, as will the fill lights and backlights. Some scenes may call for multiple fill lights, while other scenes require no fill lights at all. The amount and types of lights you use will vary greatly, but with this knowledge, you will understand where to begin.

HARD VS. SOFT LIGHTING

One of the most important decisions you will make when deciding how to light a scene is whether to use hard light or soft light. Both styles of light will instantly set a recognizable tone that your audience will feel. Once again, the tone of your scene or film will dictate what type of lighting would best help to tell the story.

Hard light casts sharp shadows and reveals the texture of surfaces. It adds a level of intensity to the look of your film. When hard light hits an object, it bounces off, which is why it creates such deep and well-defined shadows. *Be careful not to confuse low key with hard light as the two are completely different. Hard light can either be high key or low key, depending on where the light is placed.*

Soft light hides the texture of surfaces, and unlike hard light, when soft light hits an object, it wraps about the object creating much less defined shadows. Soft lighting is often referred to as beauty lighting because it gives an angelic glow, and it has the ability to hide skin blemishes. Just like hard light, soft light can be high key or low key, but the quality of light is completely different.

So how do you create hard light or soft light? The answer is simple. Believe it or not, you can look at any light fixture, and before you even turn it on, you can tell if it will be hard or soft. All you have to do is look at the size of the light. I don't mean the wattage or brightness; I mean the actual physical size of the light. Here's how

FIG. 6.30. HARD LIGHT.

FIG. 6.31. SOFT LIGHT.

it works; the bigger the light, the softer it will be. The smaller the light, the harder it will be.

Here are some examples:

A flashlight: hard or soft?	Hard
A car headlight: hard or soft?	Hard
A movie theater projector?	Hard

How about a light bouncing off a movie screen? It's soft, because even though it's the same light as the projector, once it hits the screen, it becomes much larger and softer.

How about sunlight? It's hard, even though the sun is so massive. But if you look at the sun from our perspective, it is actually quite small because of its distance from Earth. The farther away you move a light, the smaller it becomes.

How about sunlight on a cloudy day? Soft, because hard sunlight hits the clouds and spreads out as it passes through, making it a bigger light. It is no longer the size of a quarter, but rather the size of the entire sky.

This same concept is one of the key ways of turning a hard light into a soft light on set. There are actually two techniques for achieving this. The first is reflection. Shining a small light onto a larger reflective surface will create a softer light (see fig. 6.24). This

FIG. 6.32. WARM LIGHTING.

FIG. 6.33. COOL LIGHTING.

is the theory of the movie screen example. The bigger the surface you reflect off, the softer the light will be. White is the most reflective color in the color spectrum, while black reflects no light at all. If you choose to bounce light off other colors, be aware that there will be less light, and the light you reflect will take on the color of the reflector you are using. For example, if you bounce light off a red wall, it will reflect red light. This is not necessarily a negative; it is simply something to be aware of. Another important thing to remember is that the light source you are using to create the reflected light is no longer your light source. Your light source is now the reflector. This means you must place the reflector where you want your light to be coming from.

The second technique for turning a hard light into a soft light is to diffuse the light. This is the sunlight-through-the-clouds example. Shining a hard light through something translucent will spread out the light and soften it (see fig. 6.25). If you shine a hard light through a clear window, it will still be a hard light because a window is transparent. If you shine it through a frosted glass window, it will become a soft light because the frosted glass is translucent.

We have many tools on set to create varying levels of softness. One tool often used when shooting exteriors are large "silks." These silks are large squares of thin white fabric that attach to a large metal frame. These range in size from 4' × 4' up to 40' × 40' and larger. Cinematographers will often hoist these large squares of fabric into the air above a scene to soften the harsh sunlight.

Because the fabric is translucent, it creates a soft glow beneath the silk. This can also be achieved on a much smaller scale. Silks can be found in smaller sizes like 18" × 24" or 24" × 36" and are often placed in front of lights when shooting interior scenes. This will result in the exact same effect. Both reflection and diffusion will result in a significant loss of brightness, so make sure you have a bright enough light when you begin.

COLOR

In chapter 4 we discussed the different color temperatures and what type of light creates each color. In this chapter, we will discuss color from a lighting standpoint instead of from the camera's perspective.

One of the most important decisions a director, cinematographer and production designer will make is what colors to use in their film. This is not something that is decided when you arrive on set; this is a decision that is made well in advance of ever stepping foot on set. In fact, in the pre-production process there will be many discussions about the look and color palette of the film. The color palette is the range of colors that appear in the film. You, as a filmmaker, may decide your film requires vibrant colors like reds and oranges, with a splash of green. That is your color palette. You may decide that your film calls for muted tones like beiges or gray tones. That is also a color palette. Color palettes can also vary from scene to scene in the same film.

Every film will be different, but it is essential that all crew members are creating a unified look for the film. One way to ensure that all creative crew members are on the same page is to create a "visual notebook" or "look book." A look book is a binder that you create filled with images that represent the look of the movie. There are no rules to creating a visual notebook, other than to make sure when a person looks through it they understand the look of the film. One common technique is to get paint swatches to show the colors you plan on using for the film. Look books can also contain wardrobe or locations, as well as types of light (hard or soft, low key or high key). I cannot tell you how many times I've been on set and the director and I are having a difficult time achieving the look we want. Oftentimes we will go back to the visual notebook, and after a quick viewing, we are able to work through the problem. Describing how you want a film to look can be a real challenge, so having something tangible like a photograph or color swatch can be tremendously useful.

Color choice should never be a haphazard decision. Colors almost always represent an emotion, and although the audience may not be conscious of this, subconsciously they can certainly feel it.

One interesting note: Colors mean different things in different cultures. Here is a list of colors and their meanings in western society.

Black—Negativity, mystery, sadness, evil, power, sexuality, sophistication, elegance, fear

Blue—cold, tranquility, calm, contentment, depression, unity, trust, truth, confidence, sky, water, technology

Brown—earth, home, comfort, outdoors, simplicity, reliability, stability

Gold—wealth, prosperity, grandeur, extravagance

Green—health, sickness, perseverance, tenacity, environment, spring, fertility, envy

Orange—warmth, enthusiasm, humor, energy, balance

Pink—love, romance, feminine, innocence, playfulness, delicate

Purple/Violet—enlightenment, spirituality, royalty, nobility, wisdom, cruelty, arrogance

Red—danger, anger, passion, heat, violence, rage, desire, power, love, aggression, fire, blood

Silver—riches, glamorous, high-tech, sleek, elegant

White—Positivity, innocence, good, love, purity, simplicity, cleanliness, peace, youth, birth, winter, snow (Eastern cultures), death

There are many different ways to achieve the desired color in your film. One of the best approaches is to place gels over the lights. Gels are colored sheets of plastic that change the color of the light to whatever color gel you use. This will allow you to change the color of specific lights rather than the entire image. If you are trying to change the entire look of the image, the best approach is to use filters in the camera or adjust your white balance. Filters are pieces of glass that attach to the front of the camera lens and can change everything from the color to the texture. They can soften the image to give a dreamlike effect; they can add clouds to the sky or block glare from windows.

You can and should also choose the degree of color you actually have. Color is measured in saturation and the more saturation you have, the more vibrant the colors can be. When all of the saturation is removed, the image becomes black and white. Many films that take place in different time periods throughout history choose a very desaturated look, bordering on black and white, but not quite black and white. This adds a sense of nostalgia to a film, which can really lend itself to films that are set in the 1930s and 1940s. When a filmmaker wishes to give a whimsical or animated feel to his film, they can boost the saturation and create a world that is more vivid than reality.

HOW TO LIGHT

I still remember the first time I tried to light a scene. I took out all my lights, put them on stands, plugged them in and pointed them at the actors face. Why? I have no idea. I just thought that's what you are supposed to do. I see many new filmmakers making the exact same mistake. This lead me to create a checklist that I still use to this day.

THE FOUR QUESTIONS OF LIGHTING

When I was a young cinematographer, I often felt overwhelmed by the amount of lighting possibilities. You can essentially place your lights anywhere, so how do you decide what the correct positioning is? I narrowed my concerns down to four areas, then devised questions to address these areas. I began asking myself these four questions before I set up any lights. Since then, I've never again wondered where to place a light. The answers to these four questions, while generic, will give you all of the information you need.

The first step, before we get to the questions, is to realize that you are trying to recreate reality. All of the lights you are placing should have the same goal, to look realistic and believable. When I say realistic, I don't mean they have to look like reality, but they do have to match the reality of the world you have created.

Question #1: Where would my light be coming from, in reality? This is, by far, the most important question. If a person is sitting in a dark room and they turn on a lamp that is on their right side, and the left side of their face is brighter, something is wrong. You must know what your key light is supposed to be mimicking in the reality of the film and act as if that is what is lighting your scene. If a person is standing in front of a window and the scene takes place during the day, there has to be daylight coming in through the window. But films are often shot on soundstages where there is no natural light. It is the job of the cinematographer to make it appear that there is daylight coming in through the window. When you arrive on set, take some time, walk the set and truly consider, *"If this was reality, where would the light come from?"*

Question #2: What type of light would it be?

If you can answer question #1, you can answer this question as well. Just ask yourself, "What would the real light source be?" Then remember the rule that a small light is hard and a large light is soft. If the light is supposed to be the sun, it should be hard light. If the light source is supposed to be overhead fluorescent lights, the light should be soft. Lighting will often be a combination of both hard and soft light. For example, if your scene consists of a person sitting on a couch in a living room, there are many choices for how to light that scene. In our scenario, there will be a large window with direct sunlight on one side of the subject and a white wall on the other side. Should you light the scene with hard light or soft light? The answer is . . . *both!* The direct sunlight will need to be hard light because we know that direct sunlight is hard. However, you can light the opposite side of their face with soft, bounced light to fill in the shadows because the large white wall will justify it. You may actually get enough bounced light from the key light (fake sun through the window) but if you don't, you can supplement the fill light by bouncing a light off the wall. One of the most common combinations is a hard key light and a soft fill light, but any combination of hard and soft will work, as long as it's representative of your set's physical layout.

Question #3: How much light would there be?

We all know how bright daylight, moonlight, or a desk lamp is; remember that when lighting your scene. If the amount of light you use to light a scene doesn't match the light source, it seems unrealistic. The audience is not savvy enough to understand what the problem is, but they are savvy enough to know there is a problem. If you light a match in a pitch black room and the entire space lights up, it won't look believable. Just think about what reality would look like.

Question #4: What color would the light be?

We have discussed that daylight is blue, tungsten lights are orange, and fluorescent lights are most often green. If you know what would be creating your light, you should know what color it is. That doesn't mean you can't get creative with your colors; just find a way to justify your choices. How often in reality do you see a person being lit by red light? If you want to use red lights, show what is creating that red light. It could be a stop light, a car taillight, or a neon sign, but whatever source you decide to use, show it to the audience. Think creatively, but know that the audience will wonder what's casting that glowing red light.

PRACTICAL LIGHTS

As we discussed in the previous four questions of lighting, it is important to justify where your light is coming from. When lights are arbitrarily placed, it seems artificial and the audience will often be aware that something doesn't look right. One way of explaining where your light is coming from is by using practical lights. A practical light is any light that can be seen within the frame.

If your practical light is bright enough to actually light the scene, that can be helpful, but it doesn't have to actually be creating the light in the scene. It is perfectly acceptable to have another light out of the frame creating the actual light that the audience will believe is coming from the practical light. As long as it appears that the light is coming from the practical light, the audience will believe it. Similarly, if you are using desk lamps or something similar to light a scene, but they don't appear in the frame, they are not practical lights. It must be seen in the frame to be considered a practical light.

Practical lights are a valuable tool, but there are a few guidelines you should follow when incorporating them into any scene, especially when using a secondary light to enhance the practical light.

1. The subject should not be brighter than the practical light. This only applies if you are using a secondary light to supplement the output of the practical light. If your secondary light is too bright, it will make the person being lit brighter than the light that is supposedly lighting them. That creates a major believability issue.

2. The direction of secondary light must match that of the practical light. Wherever your practical light is positioned in the frame, the secondary light must come from the same direction. Once again, this only applies if you are using a secondary light to supplement the practical light.

3. The color of the secondary light must match that of the practical light. If you are using a practical light that has a distinct color, such as warm Edison bulbs, or a lamp with a colored shade, the supplemental light hitting the subject must be the identical color. This can be accomplished by using gels on the secondary light to mimic the color of the practical light.

CHOOSING A TIME OF DAY TO SHOOT

One of the most important skills a cinematographer must possess is knowing what time of day to shoot. There have been several Academy Award–winning films that used only natural light for exterior shots, such as *Children of Men*, *The Thin Red Line*, and *Barry Lyndon*. The reason for this is that natural daylight is, in my opinion, the most beautiful light source available. It is also the most difficult to control. The best you can hope for is to have enough knowledge to make the sunlight work for you. Each time of day will have a unique look. It is up to you, as a filmmaker, to choose the look that works for your film.

SUNRISE/MORNING

When the sun first begins to rise, the sky will glow before you can see the actual sun, resulting in a cold pale glow. As the sun gets closer to the horizon, the color will turn from blue to orange.

Sunrise: Dawn is a beautiful time of day to shoot because the warm color temperature can be exquisite. Because of the angle of the sun, you will have quite a bit of contrast and shadows. The sun is also not at its brightest point yet, so it is far easier to create contrast and balanced exposure.

Morning: As the sun gets higher in the sky, it will start to turn back toward the blue end of the spectrum. This is a great time of day to shoot because it looks like the middle of the day to the camera without the issues we will discuss with midday. Morning will last for different lengths depending on the time of year, but will generally end between 10 and 11 a.m.

MIDDAY

For most types of shooting, midday is the worst time of day to shoot. The sunlight is incredibly intense and compensating for it is difficult. It is simply too bright for most types of cameras. Because of the angle of the sun, there is very little contrast. All of the shadows will be at the actor's feet. Another major issue with shooting during midday is that people get deep eye-socket shadows. Shooting during midday is the equivalent of top lighting, which means that light cannot get into the eyes. This is a very unattractive look. It is possible to shoot during midday; however, to achieve a balanced look, it is often necessary to use tools such as large silks, reflectors and lens filters.

AFTERNOON/SUNSET

The perfect time of day to shoot if you want the look of midday without the challenges.

Afternoon: Between 3 and 4 p.m., as the sun starts to move lower in the sky, its intensity will begin to dissipate, and it will no longer be directly overhead. The contrast will return, and the shadows will be at a much more pleasing angle. The sky will still be blue, but there is a little bit of warmth that is added to the color. One of the best techniques for shooting during this time of day is to put the sun behind your subjects as a backlight and use a reflector to bounce the sunlight onto their faces. This creates a beautiful glowing light in the subject's hair, and the reflector gives a warm, soft glow to the skin.

Sunset: When the sun gets lower in the sky, it begins to turn to sunset. This is not just the five minutes before the sun is gone. This time period begins when orange begins to dominate the blue of the sky. This is the second most beautiful time of day to shoot because of the warm glow, heavy shadows, and lower intensity of light. It is often much warmer than sunrise and a favorite of most cinematographers. Just be aware that this time period does not last long, perhaps an hour to ninety minutes depending on the time of year. The light is also softest during this period because of the angle of the sun.

MAGIC HOUR

This is the final time period of the day. If you aren't familiar with magic hour, it is that time of day after the sun has gone below the horizon, but the sky is still glowing. It is called magic hour because of the magical quality of the light. It is warm and incredibly soft. In fact, there are no shadows anywhere. The sky becomes a giant soft-box. I cannot tell you how many directors I have met that pitch me the idea of shooting a feature film that takes place at magic hour. My response is always the same thing. "Great! I hope you have five years to shoot your film."

Magic hour is indeed beautiful. It is the most picturesque time of day, but completely impractical for long scenes. Magic hour at its longest lasts for an hour, but during winter months is as short as twenty minutes. Magic hour's best use is for short, visually striking scenes, not for scenes with large amounts of dialogue.

Cinematography is one of the most complex and technical elements of any film. Many of the great cinematographers throughout the history of film have devoted their lives to unlocking the secrets of light and shadow. There are few arts that require as much time, devotion, and patience as lighting, but there are also few as rewarding. Lighting has the ability to transform any scene and inform the audience in ways no other elements can. Mastering it can take a lifetime, and this chapter is in no way going to make you an expert. We are just scraping the surface of the surface in this chapter, but I hope it will give you a basic understanding of what is involved. These techniques and concepts should give you a strong starting point and enough knowledge to begin your experimentation. Remember, the only way to truly master lighting is to light.

CHAPTER 7

DRAWING THE AUDIENCE'S EYE

One of the biggest challenges a filmmaker faces is ensuring that the audience is focused exactly where you need them to be at all times. If something in the frame is drawing the audience's eye to the wrong point, they may miss important elements of the film. This might be minor or it could lead to great confusion amongst your audience, the latter of which could be catastrophic to your film.

Keeping the audience's attention for a ten-minute short film is extremely challenging, but keeping them focused for a two-hour feature film is nearly impossible! That being said, it's done all the time. So how do you ensure the audience is focused on the correct point of the frame? There are several techniques that we use to draw the audience's eye. We will discuss six in this chapter, and we will cover them in order of significance and effectiveness. Before we delve into the techniques, I want you to understand that just like all of the other elements we have discussed, these techniques carry a great amount of visual weight. They must be used cautiously and appropriately in order to make them invisible to the audience. The biggest mistake you can make is assuming the audience isn't savvy enough to understand the visual suggestions you have given them. This mistake will lead to the creation of heavy-handed images. The audience doesn't need to be force fed; they simply need to be guided. By using just a few subtle techniques, we can direct the audience without them being acutely aware.

Allowing the audience to feel as though they have deciphered a riddle is always the goal. It will create a much more satisfying movie-going experience for the audience. They feel like active participants in the film, rather than passive observers. One of my favorite examples of this is the ending of the film *The Usual Suspects*. As an audience member, you actually feel as though you are solving the mystery of the film in real time, when in reality, the director is giving you all of the information you need in the exact order you need it.

There are many advanced techniques at work in that film, but in order to use such techniques appropriately, we must first start with the basics. Once you are able to master the use of these six techniques, the quality of your images will increase exponentially and the audience will feel far more engaged.

SIX ESSENTIAL TECHNIQUES

1. Exposure
The first technique for drawing the audience's eye is to use exposure. The human eye will always be first drawn to the brightest point in the frame. Even if the brightest point in the frame has no significance, we have no choice but to look there first; our brain won't allow us to do otherwise. It instantly grabs our attention. If you don't believe me, give this a try: Pause a frame of a TV show or movie. Swing your head quickly to the screen, then

FIG. 7.1 THE EYE WILL BE DRAWN TO THE BRIGHTEST POINT IN THE FRAME.

quickly away. Do this a few times in rapid succession and see where your eye is drawn first. I can almost guarantee it will be drawn to the brightest point in the frame. So how do you use this to your advantage? It's pretty simple. Make your point of interest the brightest point in the frame. If your character is lit brighter than the rest of the frame, the audience's eye will be drawn to them instantly. This technique will avoid any confusion or distraction for the audience.

Just like any other rule, this one is meant to be broken. There are many circumstances where you might not want your point of interest to be the brightest part of the frame. For example, if you have a practical light in your frame, it might not make sense for the actor to be more brightly lit than the light source.

FIG. 7.2. IT IS NOT ALWAYS POSSIBLE TO MAKE YOUR SUBJECT THE BRIGHTEST POINT IN THE FRAME.

FIG. 7.3. WHEN HIDING YOUR SUBJECTS IN SHADOW, SOMETHING IN THE FRAME SHOULD STILL BE PROPERLY EXPOSED.

Another example is a character hiding in the shadows. It would be quite difficult to have a character hiding in the shadows if she is brightly lit, so making her the brightest point in the frame would not work. In situations like this, you must still have a bright point in your frame to inform the audience that the character is in the shadows. This gives the audience a reference as to what proper exposure is, showing them that your character is not in the light.

Many cinematographers will often place something black and something white within every frame as an exposure reference. This is not a necessity but rather a stylized choice. In situations like hiding a character in the shadows, you have to find a way of drawing the audience away from the brightest point of the frame and to your point of interest. Although exposure is the first approach for drawing the audience's eye, it is not the only technique. The second technique would be much more appropriate for situations like this.

2. Focus

Although the audience will still be drawn to the brightest point of the frame first, they will be drawn to whatever is in focus for the longest period of time. If the brightest point is out of focus, they will immediately look there, then quickly look away to whatever

FIG. 7.4. FOCUS IS AN EFFECTIVE TOOL FOR GUIDING THE AUDIENCE'S EYE.

FIG. 7.6. A FOLLOW FOCUS IS USED TO SHIFT FOCUS ON THE LENS.

FIG. 7.5. SHIFTING FOCUS WILL SHIFT THE AUDIENCE'S ATTENTION.

FIG. 7.7. THE 1ST ASSISTANT CAMERAPERSON (1ST A. C.) SHIFTS THE FOCUS AS THE SCENE CHANGES.

is in focus. Our brains will not allow us to look at an out-of-focus image for very long, so we will automatically seek out proper focus. Using a shallow depth of field (discussed in chapter 4) can be a great technique for guiding the audience's eye to a particular point.

You can also use focus to shift the audience's perspective during the scene simply by shifting the focus. In figures 7.4 and 7.5, focus is shifted from the girl in the foreground to the boy in the background. This will cause the audience to adjust where they are looking because our eye will search for focus.

This technique is as simple as turning the follow focus, which is a device that connects to the focus ring on the lens or turns the focus ring on the lens directly (see figures 7.6 and 7.7).

A deep depth of field is ideal for allowing the audience to examine the entire frame, but for the moments where you need the audience to look at one particular point, a shallow depth of field can be extremely effective. Also, keep in mind that the depth of field does not need to be the same for every shot in the scene. It is perfectly acceptable to have a deep depth of field in one shot and a shallow depth of field for the next shot. A shallow depth of field is useful for reaction shots, while a deep depth of field may be better for master shots or group shots. Of course, you are free to use any depth of field with any type of shot. Once again, there are no mandatory requirements.

3. Movement

We will always be drawn to anything that is moving in the frame. This technique can certainly be paired with other elements to create an image that is impossible to look away from, but it will not overpower focus, so if you want movement to draw the eye, it works best when in focus. It doesn't have to be the brightest point in the frame. Even if it's darker than other points in the frame, the movement will grab our attention.

Movement is also a great way of masking camera moves and for getting from one location to another. You will often see films where the camera follows a person that is not part of the story in order to get to another space. Motivating camera movement can be a daunting task, but we will cover that in chapter 8.

FIG. 7.8. MOVEMENT WILL GRAB THE AUDIENCE'S ATTENTION.

4. Color

As we discussed in the lighting chapter, each color has a complementary color. When these two colors are combined, they make each other stand out. For example, if you have an image that is primarily blue and you place something orange in the frame, the audience will be drawn to the orange because it will look so out of place. Combining complementary colors is a great way of drawing the eye while still being subtle. Certain colors have more power than others; the color red is the most dominant color in the spectrum. Red will always draw the eye, especially when it is paired with its complementary color green or when contrasted with black or white.

Red can be extremely effective, but be aware that too much red can be difficult to watch. It should be used sparingly and deliberately.

When shooting a black-and-white film, you obviously don't have the luxury of complementary colors, so you have to rely heavily on contrast. The eye will be drawn to areas of high contrast just like it is drawn to complementary colors.

5. Frame Within a Frame

Another way of drawing the audience's eye to a particular point of the frame is to create a frame within a frame. This means you are creating a secondary frame within the frame of the movie. This can be done any number of ways: shooting through a window or doorway, using people, objects or location, or even by the use of shadows. There are many times you might want to have a wide shot or feel distant from a character, but in a wide shot, there are too many possibilities for the audience's eye to be drawn. A

FIG. 7.9. THE RED DRESS GRABS THE AUDIENCE'S ATTENTION.

FIG. 7.10. TWO SOLDIERS CREATE A FRAME WITHIN A FRAME.

FIG. 7.11. DOORWAY CREATES A FRAME WITHIN A FRAME.

FIG. 7.12. SIGN DRAWS THE AUDIENCE'S ATTENTION.

frame within a frame allows you to draw attention to something or someone without having to show it in a close-up. It leaves little confusion as to where the audience should look.

6. Words

Anytime we see words on screen, we will read them. Not only will we read them, but we will actually read them over and over again without even knowing it, especially if the frame changes, yet the words are still there. When I say words, I'm not talking about subtitles. I am talking about words on a sign or graffiti on a wall. This can either work for you or against you. If the placement of a sign is intentional and it carries a message, it can be extremely helpful. For example, if a character is making bad decisions, a strategically

placed "danger" sign can add a wonderful bit of subtext. However, if there is a billboard for a dentist in the background, and it has nothing to do with your film, it can be extremely distracting.

These six techniques are just the beginning when it comes to drawing the eye, but they are a great place to start. You will come across dozens of other techniques as you progress in your filmmaking career, but these six methods are tried and tested. I find myself returning to them time and time again. Remember, when designing a frame, it is your responsibility to make sure you are informing the audience and guiding their eye. When done correctly, you will create a seamless image with no distractions or confusion.

CHAPTER 8

CAMERA MOVEMENT

One of the most important elements of directing and cinematography is camera movement. Although technique is important, we will focus our attention on motivation because understanding when and why to move the camera is far more significant. Possessing the ability to operate a camera smoothly is crucial; however, that is something that comes with experience, and just like riding a bike, the more you practice, the smoother it will be. I highly recommend that you shoot as often as possible. Camera operation is muscle memory, and eventually, it will become second nature.

Camera movement is a powerful tool, and when motivated, it will drastically increase the power of a scene. Moreover, it can help to envelop the audience and draw them into the world of the story. When camera movement is unmotivated it draws attention to itself and pulls the audience out of their cinematic trance. The goal is to create camera movements that are invisible to the audience. That will often prove to be a challenge, as the line between a motivated camera movement and an unmotivated camera movement is quite fine.

First, I want you to familiarize yourself with the term "conscious camera." You will hear me use this term often in this chapter. A conscious camera is when the audience becomes aware of the camera movement. It makes them acutely conscious that they are watching something that was shot on a camera. I know this seems silly, because the audience obviously knows the movie they are watching was shot on a camera, but when shot correctly, the audience slips into dream mode, which is the state where you are no longer paying attention to the fact that you are watching a movie. You become so engrossed in the film that all outside distractions disappear. A conscious camera shakes you out of dream mode, and you instantly become aware that you are watching a movie.

So how do you avoid creating a conscious camera? The first thing is to understand why you move the camera. The best motivation to move the camera is because something is changing. When I say "something," it can be almost any reason. However, the best two motivations are emotional changes and physical changes. These two motivators often call for significant visual shifts, which lend themselves to camera movement. For example, a character receiving some sort of powerful news is a great motivation for a camera move. Emotional changes are generally the best reason for moving the camera. They build on the power of the story and make us feel the emotional change a character is experiencing. You can move the camera closer to the subject to maximize the impact, or you can move the camera further away to create a sense of loneliness and isolation. These are just two of the dozens of options for camera movement in this situation.

When something physically changes within the frame, this will also give you the opportunity to change the camera position. For example, if someone walks down a hallway, we can move the camera to follow them. You can also use physical changes as an opportunity to create more tension in the scene. If someone enters the frame and walks toward our subject, the movement of the person entering the frame allows us to move the camera closer to, or further away from, our subject. It works the exact same way as emotional changes; it's just a different motivation.

So now that we know why and when we move the camera, let's discuss where we move the camera. There are many places you can move the camera, but there are a few extremely common techniques that are used numerous times on almost every production.

PUSH-IN

A push-in is when you physically move the camera closer to the subject. When done correctly, a push-in can be very impactful because the audience is so engrossed in the film, they don't realize the camera is getting closer to the subject. They do, however, feel the emotional change happening. It creates a sense of growing connection to the character. A push-in will often start as a wide shot and move into a close-up but does not have to travel that far. When using a push-in, you are telling the audience something is changing. It can signify a moment of realization for a character. For example, our character has an internal moment of clarity or makes a discovery. It can also be used to maximize emotional impact, such as when a character is experiencing an emotional

FIG. 8.1. BEGINNING OF PUSH-IN.

FIG. 8.2. END OF PUSH-IN.

shift, like feeling extreme sadness, pain, or even glee. There are many reasons to use a push-in; just remember that the audience will see it as a shift in tone.

The speed of a push-in is something that should also be closely considered. If you move too quickly, the audience will be aware of the movement; if done too slowly, the audience will not feel the dramatic impact. I like to let the emotion of the scene dictate how fast we move the camera. If the scene is of a scientist who is told the world is about to explode, you can probably get away with a pretty fast push-in. However, if the scene is of a man slowly coming to terms with the choices he has made, you are going to need to move quite a bit slower. Read the scene carefully; it will

dictate how fast to move your camera. Remember, you don't want your audience to see the push-in; you just want them to feel it.

As I mentioned before, a push-in makes us feel closer to the character. But why? Well, just as in reality, the closer you are to a person, the more connected you feel to them. If you are standing across the street from someone, chances are there is very little emotional connection. But if you are standing face to face with that person, the emotional connection becomes much stronger. These same rules apply on screen. A closer shot of a person's face creates a much stronger emotional connection than a wider shot of their entire body. In addition to the change in size, the movement toward the character makes us feel as though we are being drawn to them and their emotional space. It is as though we are magically being carried toward them.

Starting in a wide shot establishes the geography of the scene. It shows the audience where we are and what is happening. If you start the push-in just after the change begins, it will be invisible. The audience will be focused on the scene, not the camera movement. Most of the time they are completely unaware that they have traveled across the room.

PULL-OUT

The opposite type of camera movement is the pull-out. It is essentially just a push-in but done in reverse. You start in a tight shot and move the camera back to a wider shot. All of the same rules apply, but they will give the exact opposite emotional effect. When the shot is started in a close-up, we will feel a connection to the character, and as the camera moves away, we will begin to feel more and more detached.

This can also be an extremely effective technique. Often, this is used to open a scene. We see a close-up of a character, which tells us *who* the scene is about; then the camera pulls out to reveal *what* the scene is about.

FIG. 8.3. BEGINNING OF PULL-OUT.

FIG. 8.4. END OF PULL-OUT.

In many situations, either a push-in or a pull-out would create emotional impact. However, it is up to you as a director to decide what type of story you are telling. For example, let's say you are filming a scene in which a character is being told of the death of a loved one. You can start with a wide shot and push-in to a close-up. This will make us feel a strong emotional connection to a character.

You can also start in a close-up, and as the character is hearing the bad news, you can slowly pull out to a wide shot. This will make us feel detached from the character and will make the character appear alone and isolated. Both are powerful messages, but you must decide which message you are trying to convey.

Both push-ins and pull-outs carry a great amount of emotional weight. This is why they are so commonly used. Although you may not realize it, you see these moves in almost every film or television show you watch. We rarely notice them because they are so well executed; however, the more you use them, the more often you will see them in other films. The easiest way to spot them is by watching the side edges of the frame. As the move begins, you will see the edges of the frame change. Pay attention and see if you start to notice them.

PUSH-IN VS. ZOOM-IN

People often confuse these two techniques because they have a similar appearance to the untrained eye. They are, however, two completely different techniques. A push-in, as we discussed, is when you physically move the camera closer to a subject. A zoom-in is when you use the zoom of a lens to magnify the image. The distance between the camera and the subject is not changing, even though the subject is getting larger. Again, it may seem difficult to differentiate between the two, but both have completely different characteristics.

Most filmmakers, as a general rule, try to avoid using zooms, especially in place of a push-in. Zooms are often avoided because they don't look natural. In reality, we can physically walk closer to a subject, just like a push-in, but unless you've got some sort of incredible bionic eye, you can't zoom in on a person. Zooms look artificial and mechanical, and often will create a conscious camera. A zoom is basically changing a lens from wide angle, through medium focal length, all the way into telephoto, and if you remember from our chapter on lenses, the different lens focal lengths have completely different characteristics. Because of the nature of a zoom, you are continuously changing the characteristics of the lens through the entire shot. Remember, a wide-angle lens has a wide field of view, and it stretches space. As you begin to zoom in, the field of view will narrow, and the background will begin to compress. With a push-in, the characteristics will stay

FIG. 8.5. END OF PUSH-IN.

FIG. 8.6. END OF ZOOM-IN.

the same through the entire shot. The final frame of a push-in will make you feel close to the subject, while the final frame of a zoom-in will make you feel like you are looking through a telescope at a subject.

At the end of the push-in (see figure 8.5), the field of view is still wide because a wide-angle prime lens was used. You can also see the forced-perspective narrowing of the walkway. The object in the background looks substantially smaller than the girl in the foreground.

At the end of the zoom-in (see figure 8.6), the field of view is much narrower than with the push-in, and the girl in the foreground looks much more compressed into the background.

TRACKING SHOT

A tracking shot is when you move along with a subject while they move. This can be following behind, leading in front, or following alongside a subject as it moves. The general rule for shooting tracking shots is to move at the same speed as the subject and stop when they stop. This will ensure that the camera remains invisible. New filmmakers often tend to use static shots, but a good tracking shot allows the audience to feel as though they are a part of the scene, which keeps them more engaged. Tracking shots becomes very significant when we discuss moving master shots in our next chapter.

TECHNIQUES FOR MOVING THE CAMERA

When it comes to moving the camera, there are many different approaches a filmmaker can take. Each will have a different look and feel, and not all are suitable for every type of scene. Similar to a push-in, the amount of camera movement should be dictated by the emotion of the scene.

DOLLY SHOT

The first type of camera movement and most common technique is a dolly shot.

A dolly is a large metal sled or platform with wheels. On some, the camera mounts directly to the dolly, and often there will be seats for the camera operator and focus puller. Other dollies, called doorway dollies, require a tripod. A dolly can run along track like a train, or if the floor is smooth and flat enough, it can roll directly on the ground. A dolly is a great tool for creating an invisible camera, and when used correctly, the camera appears to float. It is extremely smooth and great for many types of shots including push-in, pull-out or tracking shots. However, it also has some limitations. Dollies can only move in straight lines or circles. If you are planning a more complicated pattern of movement, a dolly would not be an appropriate tool.

FIG. 8.7. START OF PUSH-IN.

FIG. 8.8. END OF PUSH-IN.

HANDHELD SHOT

The next type of camera movement is handheld. Handheld can come in many forms depending on the camera, but the most common type of handheld is a shoulder-mounted camera with handgrips. A good camera operator can accomplish a handheld shot and remain fairly smooth and steady. This is, however, a learned skill and takes quite a bit of practice. Although it is essential for a camera operator to be able to keep the camera steady, it is important to note that handheld camera work will never be as smooth as a dolly. In fact, you wouldn't want it to be. If smooth and steady is what you are looking for, a dolly is a better tool. One advantage of handheld vs. dolly is flexibility of movement. As I mentioned, a dolly can only go straight ahead, side to side, or in a circle. They are also very large and don't turn well. A camera operator with a handheld camera can move in any direction. They can also turn easily and fit in small spaces.

Flexibility is not the only advantage of shooting handheld. A handheld camera is very stylized and generally meant to add a level of intensity to a scene. Chase sequences or fight scenes work great when shot handheld. Many action movies are shot handheld because the director likes the frenetic look of the action. For years, it was considered unorthodox to shoot standard, static dialogue scenes using a handheld camera, but this is all changing. Many

directors prefer the realism they achieve with handheld camera work. In these situations of very little movement, the camera operator must do their best to stay as still as possible. This technique creates a look almost similar to looking out through a character's eyes. The camera moves slightly as the camera operator breathes and adjusts. The movements are very natural and feel quite organic. This style is not for everyone, but it has become very popular in the past decade. Early cameras were so large that placing them on a camera operator's shoulder was unthinkable. As cameras continue to shrink, directors and cinematographers are getting more and more imaginative as to where they can mount them.

FIG. 8.9. HANDHELD CAMERA.

STEADICAM

There are times when you need the flexibility of handheld but the smoothness of a dolly. In situations like that, a Steadicam is your best option. A Steadicam is a chest-mounted support system that rests the camera on a large spring arm. Every time the Steadicam operator takes a step, the spring arm absorbs the shock. This keeps the camera level and steady as you move. It is similar to handheld but much smoother. The image has an almost ghostly appearance, as the camera floats midair. A Steadicam can go almost anywhere and is a great tool for shots that travel long distances or make turns. I am making this sound much easier than it is. Steadicam is a very specialized trade and is actually one of the most difficult skills to learn. Most camera operators are not Steadicam operators, and almost all Steadicam operators own their own equipment. A Steadicam in the hands of an untrained operator is a surefire recipe for audience motion sickness. There are many Steadicam workshops offered by companies that sell the equipment. Most are a few days long and are quite rigorous.

BOOMING

Booming is the act of moving the camera either up or down during the shot. Booming is a great way of revealing information through visuals and a fluid way of changing the frame. There

FIG. 8.10. STEADICAM OPERATOR DANIEL STILLING, DFF.

FIG. 8.11. LOW ANGLE ON A JIB.

FIG. 8.13. HIGH ANGLE ON JIB.

FIG. 8.12. JIB BOOMED DOWN.

FIG. 8.14. JIB BOOMED UP.

are many different tools that can be used to boom the camera. Most dollies have a hydraulic lift that the camera mounts on. This lift can be raised or lowered at different speeds. Another piece of equipment designed to boom is a jib or crane. A jib only goes up and down, while a crane can extend out. Both have the capability to boom and are extremely smooth in the hands of a skilled operator.

You can also boom on a Steadicam just by having the operator lift the camera by hand, although it won't be as steady.

PAN

Panning is the act of rotating the camera horizontally. For example, if the camera is mounted on a tripod or dolly and you turn the camera to the left or right, you are panning. You can also pan handheld just by rotating your hips. The direction will often be given as "pan left" or "pan right."

TILT

Tilting is the act of moving the camera vertically. Just like panning, the camera is often mounted to a dolly or tripod, but it can be done handheld, too. This is different from booming because the height of the camera is not changing, just the angle of the

FIG. 8.15. ROTATING THE CAMERA RIGHT OR LEFT IS CALLED A *PAN*.

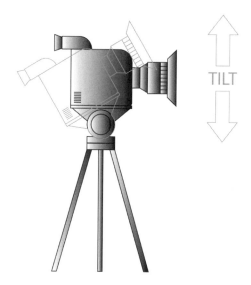

FIG. 8.16. ANGLING THE CAMERA UP OR DOWN IS CALLED A *TILT*.

lens. New filmmakers sometimes incorrectly say "pan up" or "pan down," but that is an incorrect use of the terminology. The correct direction is "tilt up" or "tilt down."

There are many new devices on the market for creating moving shots, such as drones and gimbals, and although I'd love to discuss them all, that would require its own book. As long as you understand the essentials, you possess the tools to create dynamic and thought-provoking images. In this era of gadgets, people tend to get caught up in the technology and forget about the story. Always remember that the tools are designed to support the story, not the other way around. Some of the most groundbreaking films in cinematic history were shot well before the digital era and without the aid of sophisticated camera support devices. Camera movement is an art and the masters understand that emotion should always dictate the movements.

CHAPTER 9

SHOOTING COVERAGE

Coverage is the series of shots a filmmaker shoots that will eventually be pieced together in editing to make their final film. As I'm sure you've noticed, scenes are rarely made up of just one shot. Directors compose a series of shots to maximize the emotion of the scene. Choosing these shots is one of the most important responsibilities of the director. However, every cinematographer should be just as well versed in the art of coverage. A well-trained director and cinematographer are able to create frames that will tell a strong visual story and generate a reaction from the viewer.

As with all elements of filmmaking, there is a formula to shooting coverage. Nonetheless, it is still very much an art. Shooting coverage, especially early in your career, can be intimidating and overwhelming due to the considerable number of choices one has. A camera can be placed anywhere. However, each choice will tell a different story. When done correctly, the frame will tell your story and communicate your message to the audience, but when done incorrectly, your audience may be confused or miss the meaning of the frame. Understanding what shots to choose takes a great deal of forethought and a basic understanding of psychology and human nature.

Shots are made up of many different elements, all combining to create the final product. I like to think of a shot like a car. There are many different elements that make up a car. It could be a four door and have four-wheel drive and a leather interior, or it might be a convertible with red paint and chrome wheels. A shot is similar. There are many different elements making up each shot, and it's your job to understand the effect of each element.

SHOT SIZE

The first element that makes up a shot is the size of the shot. The shot size is how large or small the subject appears in the frame. There are two different justifications for choosing a particular shot size. The first is out of necessity. If you are in a confined space, like shooting in a car, you may not be able to have a wide shot because there simply isn't enough space. Or perhaps you need to see a person head to toe to reveal their wardrobe or location, which are both common motivators for choosing a shot size. These are spatial motivators for choosing a shot size. There is, however, another reason that is equally, if not more important, which I refer to as emotional distance.

Emotional distance is how emotionally connected we feel to a subject. This emotional distance translates to actual distance on screen. As a basic rule, the closer the shot of a person we see, the more emotionally connected we feel. The farther away the shot, the less emotionally connected we feel. We touched on this in chapter 8 when we discussed push-ins. The easiest way to decide what size shot to use is to ask yourself, "How emotionally connected should the audience feel to this character at this moment?" The closer we get to the character's face, the more powerful and emotional the scene will become. If you use too many tight shots when they aren't necessary, the audience will be expecting drama that never comes. If you use too many wide shots when tighter shots are needed, the audience won't feel the power of the dramatic scenes.

In order to make an informed decision, you must first become familiar with the shot sizes. Memorizing these shot sizes is tremendously beneficial, as this is the terminology filmmakers use on set to communicate. I have also found this terminology to be largely universal. Most countries will use similar or identical terminology. This terminology makes communication on set fast and productive. For example, you will never hear a director say to a camera operator, "Frame the shot six inches above the top of the head and just below the bottom of the feet with three feet of room on each side." You are much more likely to hear a director give the instructions, "Frame up a full shot." It is a much more concise form of communication, and on-set time is at a premium.

The common misconception is that only a director and camera crew need to be familiar with this terminology. But in reality, everyone on set must know the shot sizes, whether you are a director, cinematographer, grip, wardrobe person or makeup artist. All of these crew members are part of completing the shot; therefore, they must all understand what the shot will look like. Filmmakers will often have their own preferences and variation of framing and shot sizes, but it is still much easier to tell a camera operator to "tighten up the frame" or "loosen up the frame" rather than describe exactly where you want the frame to begin and end.

FULL SHOT

A full shot (often referred to as a long shot) is a shot of a person head to toe.

FIG. 9.1 FULL SHOT.

Full shots are extremely useful for establishing geography and introducing characters because we can see where a person is positioned as well as her surroundings. It allows us to examine all of a person, which helps us gather information when first meeting a character. Although this shot size can give the audience a lot of information, it will give very little information as to the emotional state of the character. Since we are so far away from them, their face and expressions are very difficult to see. For this reason, it makes a lot of sense to start a scene in a full shot, but move into closer shots as the scene develops.

The extreme long shot is a variation where a person is extremely small in the shot and a great distance away.

FIG. 9.2 EXTREME LONG SHOT.

COWBOY SHOT

The cowboy shot is a shot size that came out of the Western era as a result of the wardrobe of the gunslingers. Full shots were too wide and didn't reflect the drama of a good old-fashion shoot-out, while the next size up was too tight to show the guns of the cowboys. Directors began splitting the difference between the two shots to compensate for the length of the holsters, and before long, a new shot size was born. This shot size gave the added drama of being closer to the character but still allowed us to see the moment a cowboy drew his weapon. In other countries, this shot size is often referred to as the "American shot" because it is so deeply rooted in America's Western movies. Although this shot size is tighter than a full shot, it is still a fairly wide shot, so there will still be minimal emotional connection with the characters.

FIG. 9.3. COWBOY SHOT.

MEDIUM SHOT

The medium shot is the most commonly used shot size in cinema because it perfectly reflects normal human interactions. It is the equivalent of the emotional distance of a typical interaction with acquaintances. For example, having an ordinary conversation with a friend or coworker is the equivalent of a medium shot. There is very little drama, but there is an inherent amount of intimacy because we are closer to the character's face. This is not the distance you would stand if approached by a stranger on the

FIG. 9.4. WIDE MEDIUM SHOT.

FIG. 9.5. TIGHTER MEDIUM SHOT.

FIG. 9.6. MEDIUM CLOSE-UP.

street, nor is it the distance if you were fighting with a friend or loved one. It is a safe, comfortable, yet familiar distance. The majority of interactions in your film will most likely be shot in this size because most movies are about real-life situations and people. Moreover, when shooting the less dramatic moments in this shot size, the more dramatic moments will become more prominent when shot in a tighter size. Medium shots are most often framed just below the waist but can also be framed just above the waist

Everything tighter than a medium shot will start to become more dramatic as the character's emotional state is on display.

MEDIUM CLOSE-UP

Medium close-ups are far more intimate than medium shots because the face is now taking up a large portion of the frame. As you start to work your way into tighter shots, make sure you are using them for the appropriate moments. A medium close-up is telling the audience that something dramatic is happening. This, in the real world, would be the equivalent of having an intimate conversation or the beginnings of an argument. It is not the most dramatic or intense shot size, but it is heading in that direction. As you move into this size shot, there are far fewer distractions for the audience. It is all about the character's emotions. As the

111

size of the character's face increases on screen, it is important to remind actors that their reactions and expressions need not be as animated as a full shot. The camera will pick up on subtle nuances that would be missed in wider shots.

CLOSE-UP

The close-up is one of the most powerful shots you have at your disposal. It is as close as you can get to a person and still show a portion of their body. Any closer than this, and it is a shot solely of the character's face. For many filmmakers, a close-up is the tightest shot they will use because on a forty-foot movie screen a character's head in a close-up will be massive. It is often said that film is a medium close-up format and television is a close-up format. This is because of the difference in screen size. A close-up on a television is far less overpowering than that on a movie screen. Although there are plenty of reasons to use a close-up, they should be used sparingly. The audience is keenly aware that when they see a close-up, something dramatic is happening. If you use this shot size when nothing dramatic is happening, the audience will believe there is some sort of subtext they should be aware of. This type of misdirection can prove to be confusing and distracting for the audience. Close-ups are powerful visual storytelling tools; just be sure to closely consider the context of the situation.

Fig. 9.7. Close-up.

TIGHT CLOSE-UP

The tight close-up is what I like to think of as the point of no return, because once you are this tight on a character's face, something dramatic has to happen. I often refer to this as the kiss or punch shot because, in reality, this is the distance you would stand away from someone if you are going to kiss them or punch them. Think about how close you would have to stand to another person to see this perspective. Of course, for the scene, those aren't the only two options, but it should carry that level of intensity. This shot is often referred to on set as a choker because it cuts off just below the chin. In this shot size, the face fills the entire frame and the character's emotions are all that matter. With the tight

FIG. 9.8. TIGHT CLOSE-UP.

FIG. 9.9. WIDER EXTREME CLOSE-UP.

close-up, you will begin to cut off the top of a person's head. As we discussed in chapter 3, this is called a "haircut." Be sure to preserve the chin in the frame as a chin dipping in and out of the picture is extremely distracting.

EXTREME CLOSE-UP

The extreme close-up is the tightest shot there is. It is rarely used these days but was very popular in '60s and '70s cinema. It is so rarely used because we rarely have that perspective in reality. We as an audience become aware that such a tight shot feels extremely uncomfortable, especially on a large screen. The extreme close-up is not an exact shot size like the others but rather a range. It begins

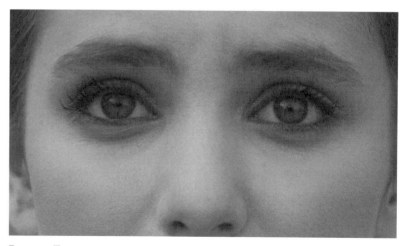

FIG. 9.10. TIGHT EXTREME CLOSE-UP.

when the eyes are framed correctly and the chin is cut off and goes all the way until just the eyes are in frame.

Although this shot size is rarely used, it should by no means be avoided. Extreme close-ups can be a powerful too, but only when they are appropriate for the scene. Just ask yourself how dramatic this moment should feel for the audience and pick your shot size accordingly.

Now that you know all of the shot sizes and how to use them, let's talk about the next element of the shot, the shot type.

SHOT TYPE

There are many different types of shots and each one carries specific information. Shot type and shot size are not mutually exclusive. The two can and do exist together in every frame. Choosing the correct shot type is just as important as choosing the correct shot size, but be sure to choose types and sizes that are telling the same story.

SINGLE SHOT

A single is pretty simple; it's a shot that contains only one person. A single can be any shot size. For example, you could have a single that is a full shot, or a single that is a close-up. The shot size in

Fig. 9.11. Clean single.

a single will help determine the emotion of the scene. The only requirement for making it a single is that it contains only one person. However, there are some variations of the single.

CLEAN SINGLE

A clean single is a true single as there is only one person in the shot. The clean single and its emptiness convey a strong emotional message; it tells the audience that the character we are seeing is alone. Not physically alone, but emotionally alone. When clean singles are used during a conversation between two people, you are telling the audience that the two people, while speaking to each other, are not emotionally connected. This can be a valuable

FIG. 9.12. CLEAN SINGLE.

FIG. 9.13. DIRTY SINGLE.

technique for showing two people who are somehow emotionally divided. For example, filming a conversation between two former lovers or a separated couple using only clean singles tells the audience that the characters are not emotionally connected. We know the two characters are speaking to each other because we can hear each one of them in the other's clean single, but the two never appear in the frame together.

DIRTY SINGLE

Similar to a clean single, a dirty single is a shot focusing primarily on one person; however, there will be a piece of another person or object. The second person is generally the character that the

FIG. 9.14. DIRTY SINGLE.

subject of the shot is interacting with. The second person in the frame is filmed in a less prominent way. We often see only a small portion of them or a nondescript part of the body like the shoulder or back of the head. The main focus of the shot will still be the person facing the camera.

A dirty single creates the exact opposite effect of the clean single; it shows a connection between the two characters. This connection doesn't necessarily have to be a positive one. Depicting a couple in love is a great time to use a dirty single, but a couple arguing works just as well. Even when people are fighting, there is still an emotional connection. If the couple no longer cares for one another and has completely emotionally shut down, clean singles would be much more effective.

OVER-THE-SHOULDER

One variation of the clean single is the over-the-shoulder. Over-the-shoulder shots are the most common and effective way to show a conversation between two people on screen. Over-the-shoulders allow us to look one character directly in the eyes but still see the person they are interacting with. The over-the-shoulder is often a two-shot sequence, one of each character in the conversation. The two shots should look almost identical. Following are some general guidelines to follow to ensure that you achieve the desired effect.

1. Use the same lens, and make sure the camera is the same distance away from the character facing the lens for both shots. This means that when you find your first over-the-shoulder, measure the distance from the camera to the subject, so you can match that distance in the reverse angle. Generally, a telephoto lens is more useful for over-the-shoulder shots.

Remember, with a wide-angle lens anything close to the lens will be very large, while anything father away will look much smaller. In an over-the-shoulder shot, the character whose back is to us is much closer to the camera, and the person who is the subject of the shot is farther away. That means that the secondary character's shoulder and back of the head will be very large, but the character who we should be focusing on is very small. This can be extremely distracting. In addition to that issue, a wide-angle lens stretches space, so the two characters will look a lot farther away from each other than they actually are.

A telephoto lens will keep the characters' heads roughly the same size in the frame as well as compress them together. This will form a strong sense of connection between the two characters.

2. Camera height does not dictate power. Yes, that's right. I know we spent quite some time discussing how the height of the camera will dictate how weak or powerful a person is, but when it comes to over-the-shoulders, this rule does not apply. The reason for that is necessity. If the more powerful character in the scene is shorter than the other character and you try to place the camera below their eye level, you will be looking at the secondary character's back, and you won't see the primary character at all.

In order to determine how high to place the camera, all you have to do is place it directly over the secondary character's shoulder. It is always nice to see a little bit of their shoulder as well as a little piece of the side of their head or ear. That, however, is just a suggestion. Feel free to frame your over-the-shoulders however you feel best tells the story.

So how will the audience know who is more powerful in over-the-shoulders? Simple; the conversation and dialogue will dictate power in the scene. Because there are two people having a conversation, how they interact with each other will give the audience a lot of information.

3. The third guideline to over-the-shoulder shots is that characters must stay on their respective sides of the frame. Once you establish where the characters are and begin the over-the-shoulders, they should stay on their side of the frame and face the same direction throughout the scene. This will help avoid confusion. For example, if character A is on the left side of the frame looking right, he must appear that way in both shots. This also means character B will be on the right side of the frame facing left and must appear that way for both shots.

FIG. 9.15. OVER-THE-SHOULDER SHOT WITH CAMERA ON BOY'S LEFT.

FIG. 9.16. REVERSE ANGLE OF FIG. 9.15, CAMERA CORRECTLY REMAINS ON BOY'S LEFT.

FIG. 9.17. OVER-THE-SHOULDER SHOT WITH CAMERA ON BOY'S LEFT.

FIG. 9.18. REVERSE ANGLE OF FIG. 9.17, CAMERA INCORRECTLY MOVES TO BOY'S RIGHT.

TWO-SHOT

A two-shot is self-explanatory; it's simply a shot that prominently frames two characters. This means that both of their faces are visible in the frame. If not, it is most likely a dirty single. Just like any shot type, the shot can be any size as long as there are two people in it. There will often be situations where the two characters will be different sizes in the frame. For example, you may have a two-shot where one character is seen in a medium shot and the other in a full shot. This is perfectly acceptable.

As you add more people to the shot, the numerical designation increases depending on how many people prominently appear in the shot—three-shot, four-shot, etc. Don't feel the need to get

FIG. 9.19. TWO-SHOT.

carried away. If you are shooting a shot of New York City's Times Square, there is no need to count heads; just call it a crowd shot.

ESTABLISHING SHOT

An establishing shot is a shot, generally wide, that shows the geography or location of the scene that will follow. It establishes where the scene takes place and oftentimes the positioning of characters, so the audience doesn't feel confused when the scene begins. If the audience spends the first few minutes of the scene trying to figure out where the characters are or where the scene takes place, they are likely to miss important information. The establishing shot doesn't need to last very long, just long enough for the audience to digest.

INSERT SHOT

There are times in a film when you want the audience to notice a particular object in frame. A ring, a note, a glass, etc. If you are filming in a wide shot, the chance of the audience noticing a wedding ring on a finger is slim to none. So how do we ensure that the audience notices the ring? Add an insert shot. An insert is a close-up of an object that appears in the frame. It's almost like saying to the audience "Hey, you! Pay attention! This is important!"

FIG. 9.20. ESTABLISHING SHOT.

FIG. 9.21. CUTTING FROM A WIDE SHOT TO A TIGHT SHOT OF AN OBJECT IN THE FRAME IS AN INSERT SHOT (SEE FIG. 9.22).

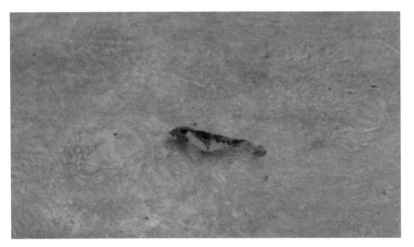

FIG. 9.22. INSERT SHOT.

CUTAWAY

A cutaway is a shot of a person or object that does not appear in the frame. For example, if a scene takes place inside of a house, cutting to the outside of the house during the scene is a cutaway. Cutaways will generally cut back to the original location and scene, but don't necessarily have to. A cutaway can serve many purposes. It can heighten tension or give the audience information that the characters don't have. It can be used to transition to a new scene, or it can help with editing. Sometimes two shots won't match well. Cutting to a shot of something else can make for a much more seamless transition. Hitchcock referred to it as the "cat in the window shot" because he used that as a cutaway to hide a bad edit in his film *Rear Window*.

Although there are many other types of shots, these are the essentials you will use most often.

SHOOTING A SCENE

There are many other types of shots, but these basics are the most commonly used during the production process. As important as it is to know your shot sizes and shot types, they mean nothing if you don't understand the actual process of shooting a scene. Recognizing what shots will best tell your story, as well as which ones can be cut together, is critical.

The most common method for shooting a scene is called the master scene technique. This method is universal and the most efficient way of shooting a scene. When followed, shooting becomes a simple formula and the risk of error is greatly minimized.

MASTER SCENE TECHNIQUE

First, you must understand what a master shot is. A master shot is a shot that covers the entire scene from beginning to end. It is generally a wide, static shot, but there are exceptions. The most important part is to ensure that you film the entire scene all in one shot.

FIG. 9.23. MASTER SHOT.

When using the master scene method, the order in which you shoot the scene is simple yet very important. First, shoot the master shot. There are a few reasons you should always shoot the master shot first. The first reason is if you film the master shot first, the entire scene is already lit and dressed. If you shoot other shots first, you might only light and dress the portions that are seen in the frame. This will create a risk of bad continuity when shooting other shots.

Another important reason for shooting the master first is you can see exactly where the actors go and what they do. This will make it extremely easy to match when shooting your coverage of the scene. Once you feel that you have gotten a few good takes of your master shot, you can move on to the coverage.

Coverage is the process of shooting the rest of the shots that will be edited together to create the scene. As we discussed, you must first shoot the master shot. It should be shot from a wide angle that will allow us to see the entire room and all of the action. Once you have shot the master, you must decide what other shots you need in order for the scene to have the dramatic effect you desire. This will most likely be shot from a few different angles and sizes. Once again, there is a protocol that should be followed to shoot this correctly. First, decide which character is to be filmed first. If you are planning on shooting multiple shot sizes of the characters, always start with the widest shot first.

FIG. 9.24. COVERAGE SHOT #1 (COWBOY).

FIG. 9.25. COVERAGE SHOT #2 (MEDIUM).

FIG. 9.26. COVERAGE SHOT #3 (INSERT).

After you have shot the widest shot size you plan to film of that character, move into the next widest shot size. Continue this until you have completed all shots.

For example, if you plan to shoot a close-up, a medium shot and a full shot of the subject, you would shoot them starting with the widest (full shot) and end with the closest (close-up) shot. You will shoot all coverage of the first character before you shoot any coverage of the second character. Next, before you move on to coverage of the other character, you should consider if you plan to shoot anything else looking the same direction as what you have just shot. This includes any insert shots you will need to make the scene complete.

Since this side of the room is already lit and dressed, you should use it. It doesn't make any sense to have to relight and dress, so you might as well get it now. This is called "shooting out" that side of the room. Once you have shot out that side of the room, you then flip the camera and shoot coverage for the other character. Remember, the reverse side of the room must now be lit and dressed. Again, you will start with the widest shot and move to the tightest shot.

This is the basic formula for shooting coverage. There are a few other important rules when it comes to shooting coverage.

1. Clean entrances and exits. This simply means to have the actors walk into the frame and hit their mark; then after they finish their

FIG. 9.27. COVERAGE SHOT #4 (REVERSE MEDIUM).

FIG. 9.29. SHOT BEGINS WITH AN EMPTY FRAME (CLEAN ENTRANCE).

FIG. 9.28. COVERAGE SHOT #5 (REVERSE MEDIUM CLOSE-UP).

FIG. 9.30. CHARACTER ENTERS FRAME (CLEAN ENTRANCE).

lines, walk out of the frame. It makes for much easier editing points, as editing on motion always looks cleanest. This rule won't always apply; in some shots, the character is already in the frame, but whenever possible, try to follow this guideline.

2. Jump two shot sizes. When choosing your shot sizes, you should generally jump at least two shot sizes between shots. For example, when shooting coverage, you would rarely shoot a full shot and a cowboy shot. A more appropriate combination would be a full shot and a medium shot. When you change shot sizes, you are telling the audience that something is happening in the scene. Changing by just one shot size is too subtle for the audience to notice and will have little to no dramatic effect. Changing by at least two shot sizes will make it much more obvious that something is actually happening.

The best way to know how many shot sizes you should change is to ask yourself how dramatic the scene is. If the scene is only slightly more dramatic, jumping two shot sizes will most likely work just fine. If a character's whole world is crumbling around them, you will want to jump quite a few shot sizes. There are no rules as to how many shot sizes you can jump. In fact, I have seen directors jump from a full shot to a close-up; just be aware of how dramatic a jump that is.

3. Change the axis of the camera. When shooting coverage, you must change the angle of the camera by at least 15 degrees between shots. For example, if your first shot is a full shot and

FIG. 9.31. CHANGE THE AXIS OF THE CAMERA BY AT LEAST 15 DEGREES TO AVOID A JUMP CUT (SEE FIG. 9.32).

FIG. 9.32. THE SLIGHT SHIFT OF THE AXIS PROVIDES A SMOOTH TRANSITION THAT WON'T STARTLE THE VIEWER.

FIG. 9.33. SHOOTING TWO SEQUENTIAL SHOTS FROM THE SAME ANGLE CREATES A JUMP CUT (SEE FIG. 9.34).

FIG. 9.34. THIS JUMP IN SPACE CAN FEEL JARRING TO THE AUDIENCE.

your next shot is a medium shot, you must change the axis of the camera between them.

The reason you must change the axis is to avoid creating a jump cut. When a wide shot and a tighter shot are filmed from the exact same angle, then edited together, it creates a jump cut. Jump cuts can be extremely jarring and noticeable.

Changing the angle of the camera will help to avoid a jump cut. You can change the axis in any direction—left, right, up or down. As a general rule, I place the widest shot farther away from the sightline of the actor, and as I move into tighter shots, I rotate in toward the eye-line. As we discussed in chapter 3, the closer we are to the eyes, the more connected we feel to the character. The same thing is true when we move closer to a character's face. Although we try to avoid jump cuts, there are some situations where jump cuts are not only acceptable, they are quite useful. Because jump cuts are so jarring, they work great when trying to startle or scare the audience. They create a similar effect to someone jumping out of a dark corner, startling the audience.

The master scene technique should always be your go-to when it comes to shooting a scene. It is efficient and effective. Another process that should always be followed is the shooting proto-col. This is the order of steps we follow leading up to the actual shooting of a scene. There are four steps that will again minimize mistakes and use time effectively.

FOUR STEPS OF THE MASTER SCENE TECHNIQUE

1. Block. Blocking is the process of finding the positions of actors and camera for shooting. A common mistake new filmmakers make is trying to light a scene before blocking. This will lead to numerous problems and drastically slow down the process. If you begin to light a scene before you position the actors, you will need to relight to ensure the actors are properly lit. No lights should be placed before blocking is complete. During the blocking process, the director and cinematographer will walk the set and find the best placement for the actors and camera. The second assistant cameraperson will follow them, putting down tape marks so the actors can easily find their places.

2. Light. Once the blocking process is complete, the cinematographer and their crew can begin lighting the scene. This is a lengthy process; in fact, the majority of the day is often devoted to lighting. Although it can seem like wasted time, remember that lighting is one of the most important visual tools we have at our disposal.

3. Rehearse. Once the scene is lit, the director and actors will rehearse the scene. This is where the director and cinematographer will see what works and what doesn't. During this process, the director and director of photography will make their final adjustments.

4. Shoot. This one doesn't really require much explanation, although you should be prepared to relight each time you change the angle of your shots.

This process is astoundingly efficient and universal. It is followed on almost all professional sets, which is one of the reasons they run like clockwork. I have also found this to be lacking on many sets run by inexperienced filmmakers. I can't stress enough how important this process is!

We now know the process of shooting coverage, but we are still only halfway

to shooting a successful scene. We have discussed shot sizes and the order in which to shoot, but we still haven't talked about where to place the camera. Camera placement is, of course, a director's prerogative and, with the help of the cinematographer, he decides where to place the camera. If the director envisions the entire scene being shot from a helicopter, that is their choice. Or if the director wants everything shot in extreme close-ups, that is also a creative decision. However, there is a basic rule that dictates where the camera can and can't be placed.

180-DEGREE RULE (THE LINE)

For many new filmmakers, this can be one of the most confusing concepts, so I will simplify it as much as possible. The line will tell you what direction to place the camera. I actually think the line simplifies things, but until you have a solid grasp of the concept, it can be extremely frustrating. This will be one of the most important concepts we cover in this chapter, so pay close attention!

First, let's talk about what the line is. Don't try to understand why quite yet; just understand how it works. The line is simply an imaginary line that is drawn from one side of the frame to the other. It is established when two characters make eye contact, or when one actor looks at something. When two characters make eye contact, the imaginary line is drawn right down the center of their bodies from one side of the frame to the other.

This will be done in the master shot. I like to think of this line as a brick wall that you cannot cross. Once you establish what side of that "wall" you are on, you cannot place the camera on the other side of it.

You must shoot all of your coverage from that side of the wall. I know this is complicated, but stay with me—it will all come together. When shooting your master shot, as soon as the characters look at each other, you have established the line. Whatever side of the line you are on is where you must stay for the rest of the scene. So, when choosing the camera position for your master

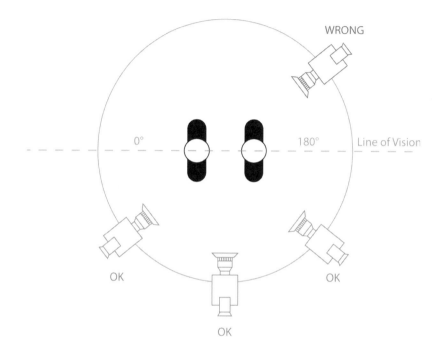

FIG. 9.35. 180-DEGREE RULE.

shot, make sure you are looking at the side of the room you wish to show. If not, you will be looking at the wrong side of the room for the rest of the scene.

Now, let's talk about why. The best analogy is to think of a basketball game. Basketball games are filmed from only one side

FIG. 9.36. CORRECT COVERAGE, CAMERA REMAINS ON THE LEFT SIDE OF THE 180-DEGREE LINE (SEE FIG 9.37).

FIG. 9.37. CORRECT COVERAGE, CAMERA DOES NOT CROSS THE 180-DEGREE LINE.

of the court. The reason is that if a player is running down the court from the left side of the camera toward the right side of the camera, he will be going that direction on TV. If you then cut to a camera on the other side of the court, the player will be running from the right side of the camera to the left side of the camera, and on TV it will look like the player is now running the opposite

direction. It creates great confusion for the audience and can be extremely distracting.

The same thing is true in film. If a character is looking screen left to screen right and you cut to the other side of the line, the character will flip flop on screen. If you are filming two people having

FIG. 9.38. INCORRECT COVERAGE, CAMERA STARTS ON THE RIGHT SIDE
OF THE 180-DEGREE LINE (SEE FIG 9.39).

FIG. 9.39. INCORRECT COVERAGE, CAMERA CROSSES TO THE LEFT SIDE
OF THE FRAME CROSSING THE 180-DEGREE LINE.

a conversation in over-the-shoulder shots and you don't obey the line, on screen it will appear that they are not looking at each other. This will confuse the audience. As shown in figures 9.40 and 9.41, it looks like the characters are looking the same direction even though when filmed the two characters were looking at each other. This is because one of the shots was filmed from the wrong side of the line.

This rule is not as restrictive as it sounds. Once you have established the line, you can travel 180 degrees in either direction. You are free to move the camera anywhere you please, as long as it is on the same side of the line.

FIG. 9.40., 9.41. BOTH SUBJECTS ARE FACING THE SAME DIRECTION ON-SCREEN WHICH DISORIENTS THE AUDIENCE.

FIG. 9.41.

BREAKING THE LINE

Although we follow the 180-degree rule, like all rules, it is meant to be broken. But also like all rules, you must break it correctly. When it comes to crossing the line, there are a few approaches that work very well. The first is to use the line cross to your advantage. Many horror films use this technique to confuse or disorient the audience. Intentional line crossing can give the audience an uneasy feeling and make it difficult to tell where characters are geographically. This lends itself to the tone of horror films.

CROSSING THE LINE

Often a director will want to show the audience different perspectives in a scene. In this case, there is a very easy way to cross the line without breaking the rules and confusing the audience. All you have to do is move the camera from one side of the line to the other during the shot without cutting. It is only confusing for the audience if you cross the line during a cut. If you show the audience how you got from one side of the line to the other, the audience won't be confused. Shooting on a dolly or handheld makes this technique very easy and invisible. This is also a great technique when you want to show the audience a different side of the characters. For example, if a character experiences an emotional change during the scene, crossing from one side of the line

FIGS. 9.42., 9.43., 9.44., 9.45., AND 9.46. CROSSING THE 180-DEGREE LINE DURING THE SHOT AVOIDS BREAKING THE 180-DEGREE RULE.

FIG. 9.44.

FIG. 9.43.

FIG. 9.45.

FIG. 9.46.

to the other can be a fantastic way of making the audience feel that change.

Obeying the 180-degree rule can be a big challenge, one that you will undoubtedly mess up. All filmmakers shoot from the incorrect side of the line at some point in their careers. Even after nearly twenty years of experience, I often find myself asking, "What side of the line are we on?" One of the most common conversations you will hear on set between a director, actor and cinematographer is what side of the camera the actor is supposed to look. It can be tremendously confusing, but slow down and ask yourself which direction the actor was looking on screen during the master shot. This will answer your question.

Shooting coverage is not something that can be learned just from reading a book, nor is it something that can be mastered after one day on set. I think coverage is one of the areas that directors struggle most with because it is such an enormous part of what a director does. Choosing the correct shots to tell your story is what gives you your voice as a filmmaker. It is how you bring your vision to life. A director should give this the weight it deserves. If you walk on set thinking that you will decide on your shots once you start shooting, you will never be able to use the shots to their full potential. A good director spends a long time in pre-production deciding what shots are needed to tell their story fully. They read the script over and over again, visualizing the scene in their head and deciding what shots communicate the story. Creating a shot list is a great technique that many directors use to ensure they don't miss anything. Most directors don't start their careers designing brilliant and elaborate shots. That is something that comes with time and experience.

One thing to remember is that while coverage is essential, it should sometimes be used sparingly. Too often, directors use too much coverage. Changing shot sizes is important, but it doesn't always have to be done through cutting. Consider changing your blocking rather than editing. A well-designed shot is almost always more effective than over-editing. The best directors are the ones that try to maximize their shots and create interesting and dynamic sequences. Moving your camera and actors will almost always be the best choice.

CHAPTER 10

CONCLUSION

Now that you have finished reading this book, you should have a solid foundation on which to begin using visual storytelling to build your voice as a filmmaker. Although there is still much to learn, you now have more than enough knowledge to begin shooting, and the more you shoot, the better your films will become. After nearly twenty years of professional filmmaking, I still find every production to be a challenge. On nearly every shoot, I still deal with unique issues and problems that must be solved. Although in the beginning of your career these challenges may seem discouraging, remember that each challenge is an opportunity to hone your skills. Soon you will no longer see them as challenges at all, but rather chances to be innovative and create new techniques.

Although a film may begin with a great script, it is the responsibility of the director and cinematographer to bring that script to life using visual storytelling. As filmmakers, we always strive to create dynamic images. However, our focus should always be to create images that both inform the audience and match the tone of the film. Every decision we make as filmmakers communicates an immense amount of information to the audience. It is our responsibility to ensure it is the correct information. Study and apply the rules we have discussed in this book . . . then break those rules every opportunity you get. Just be sure to break them with purpose. Don't be afraid to experiment; after all, that is how you will find your voice as a filmmaker.

Lastly, always remember why you decided to become a filmmaker. For me, it was a deep passion for telling stories. Your reason may be different, but remembering why you fell in love with film will get you through some very difficult times as a filmmaker. Your passion will keep you motivated and guide your voice. Always remember that passion leads to inspiration and inspiration is where the magic of film is born. A strong understanding of visual storytelling will help you harness that magic.

ABOUT THE AUTHOR

ABOUT THE AUTHOR

Morgan Sandler is a professor of Digital Film Production at the University of La Verne in Southern California. Although he teaches a wide array of classes, he specializes in film production and theory. His love of visual storytelling and creating powerful images guides his teaching and curriculum as does his passion for education. Before accepting his position at the University of La Verne, Sandler helped design the Digital Cinematography program at California State University, Los Angeles, where he also served as an adjunct professor. He previously served as the Course Director of Cinematography at The Los Angeles Film School, where he taught for ten years helping to shape many courses and design a large portion of the curriculum.

In addition to his teaching, Sandler has spent nearly twenty years working professionally as a cinematographer and camera operator for the film and television industries, which he continues to do when outside of the classroom. His passion for film is second only to his love of teaching.

Sandler holds an M.F.A. in Film, Television and Theatre from California State University, Los Angeles.

I would love to hear from you. Please email me at msandler@laverne.edu

THE MYTH OF MWP

In a dark time, a light bringer came along, leading the curious and the frustrated to clarity and empowerment. It took the well-guarded secrets out of the hands of the few and made them available to all. It spread a spirit of openness and creative freedom, and built a storehouse of knowledge dedicated to the betterment of the arts.

The essence of the Michael Wiese Productions (MWP) is empowering people who have the burning desire to express themselves creatively. We help them realize their dreams by putting the tools in their hands. We demystify the sometimes secretive worlds of screenwriting, directing, acting, producing, film financing, and other media crafts.

By doing so, we hope to bring forth a realization of 'conscious media' which we define as being positively charged, emphasizing hope and affirming positive values like trust, cooperation, self-empowerment, freedom, and love. Grounded in the deep roots of myth, it aims to be healing both for those who make the art and those who encounter it. It hopes to be transformative for people, opening doors to new possibilities and pulling back veils to reveal hidden worlds.

MWP has built a storehouse of knowledge unequaled in the world, for no other publisher has so many titles on the media arts. Please visit www.mwp.com where you will find many free resources and a 25% discount on our books. Sign up and become part of the wider creative community!

Onward and upward,

Michael Wiese
Publisher/Filmmaker